Air-to-Ground Battle for Italy

MICHAEL C. MCCARTHY
Brigadier General, USAF, Retired

Air University Press
Maxwell Air Force Base, Alabama

August 2004

Air University Library Cataloging Data

McCarthy, Michael C.
    Air-to-ground battle for Italy / Michael C. McCarthy.
        p. ; cm.
    Includes bibliographical references and index.
    ISBN 1-58566-128-7
    1. World War, 1939–1945 — Aerial operations, American. 2. World War, 1939–1945 — Campaigns — Italy. 3. United States — Army Air Forces — Fighter Group, 57th. I. Title.

    940.544973—dc22

Disclaimer

Opinions, conclusions, and recommendations expressed or implied within are solely those of the author and do not necessarily represent the views of Air University, the United States Air Force, the Department of Defense, or any other US government agency. Cleared for public release: distribution unlimited.

Air University Press
131 West Shumacher Avenue
Maxwell AFB AL 36112-6615
http://aupress.maxwell.af.mil

Contents

Chapter		Page
	DISCLAIMER	ii
	FOREWORD	v
	ABOUT THE AUTHOR	vii
	PREFACE	ix
	INTRODUCTION	xi
	Notes	xiv
1	GREAT ADVENTURE BEGINS	1
2	THREE MUSKETEERS TIMES TWO	11
3	AIR-TO-GROUND BATTLE FOR ITALY	45
4	OPERATION STRANGLE	65
	INDEX	97

Photographs follow page 28

Foreword

The events in this story are based on the memory of the author, backed up by official personnel records. All survivors are now well into their eighties. Those involved in reconstructing the period, the emotional rollercoaster that was part of every day and each combat mission, ask for understanding and tolerance for fallible memories.

Bruce Abercrombie, our dedicated photo guy, took most of the pictures. My brother-in-law, Chuck Lynch, recovered much of their original clarity. Paul Carll, with the best mind of any of us for names, dates, and details of daily events, also helped in many ways. I absolve them of any responsibility for mistakes in this work.

Four sons and seven daughters each had a hand in convincing me to tell this remarkable story. But three wonderful people in my life were particularly effective in motivating me to begin and, especially, to finish the job. They are my son Jerry, daughter Maureen, and my lovely wife, Eileen, who tolerated no procrastination.

MICHAEL C. McCARTHY
Brigadier General, USAF, Retired

About the Author

Born in Boston, Massachusetts, the oldest of six with five sisters, this first-generation Irish-American signed up for the Aviation Cadet program after Pearl Harbor. He survived the testing process and completed pilot training on 4 January 1943, as a 21-year-old second lieutenant with silver wings, new gold bars on his shoulders, and an assignment to Sarasota, Florida, to learn how to fly and operate the P-40 weapon system in a combat environment.

In April 1943, this combat-ready fighter pilot joined the 57th Fighter Group southeast of Tunis on the Cape Bon peninsula. He stayed with that distinguished air-to-ground fighter group until May 1945. The air-to-ground battle for Sicily and Italy was the focus of daily combat operations. German defenses extracted a fearful price from those Allied fighter forces whose mission was to attack and destroy them.

The arrival late in 1943 of the P-47 Thunderbolt made it possible to win the air-to-ground war and enabled many to survive to tell the story. This is his story of two years in that environment with his classmates from the first big post-Pearl Harbor pilot training class, 43-A.

Preface

Pearl Harbor galvanized America to convert peacetime production capacity to war levels, intensify recruiting, and expand every facet of its military training system. Those of us who wanted to fly found on Monday, 8 December 1941, that a difficult written test would satisfy the two years of college prerequisite to enter the Aviation Cadet aircrew-training program. We still faced a rigorous physical exam and batteries of psychological and intelligence evaluations plus specific aptitude tests. The process was intense, demanding, and time consuming. Only 41 survivors of several hundred original applicants in the Boston area became aviation cadets on 18 March 1942. Five days later, we reported to Santa Ana Army Air Base, California, for preflight training—the first of four phases en route to pilot, navigator, or bombardier wings.

Santa Ana was a new base with no roads or buildings. Tents were used for every purpose. The wettest rainy season in years converted the base into a muddy quagmire. Amazingly, the program stayed on schedule despite almost impossible living and working conditions. I found a remarkable can-do attitude to be characteristic of Army personnel in every step of the training process.

Our class opened a new primary flight school in Scottsdale and a new basic flight school in Marana, both in Arizona. Neither was ready for occupancy, but the Army made do and opened on time, producing graduates who met course completion standards despite obvious handicaps. On 4 January 1943, Class 43-A graduated from Luke Field on schedule with more than 400 new pilots. Other advanced flying bases produced similar numbers to provide a steady flow of young Americans to support theater requirements for combat aircrews.

Operational P-40 training in Sarasota, Florida, started two weeks later. The schedule provided the necessary 40 hours for each of us in eight weeks. By the end of March, we reported to Dale Mabry Field, Tallahassee, Florida, for overseas processing. With our gear, we boarded a new four-engine C-54 for Africa via Miami, Trinidad, Belem, Ascension Island, and Accra. Many of us volunteered to ferry P-40s from Lagos (down the coast from

Accra) through equatorial Africa to Cairo—an unlikely saga, completed successfully—without maps or navigational aids. That ferry trip was the first example of an indomitable can-do determination to complete the mission. That attitude became the defining characteristic of leadership philosophy in the 57th Fighter Group. Those selected for positions of greater responsibility had to demonstrate leadership capability—the ability to think under pressure and the determination to get the job done.

The last two chapters focus on highlights of the more memorable missions that took place during two years of bitter fighting between implacable enemies—one who never gave ground willingly, and one who never quit trying to find a better way to get the job done. For the most part, the events are accurate accounts with due allowance for fallible memories of participants who have survived some 60 years since these events demanded and received complete concentration from all who were part of the 57th Fighter Group. At a recent gathering of old fighter pilots, everyone agreed with the sequence of the missions but each of us had a different memory of where we were flying in the formation.

Introduction

World War II produced countless soldiers', sailors', and airmen's stories. All of these personal accounts have some value, but few of them saw the light of day. Keeping a diary was strictly against regulations (not that this stopped everyone), and most returning vets preferred to forget the war and focus on the opportunities offered by the GI Bill and the postwar boom. Few took the trouble to put pen to paper and revisit traumatic and life-altering times. Some of the resulting efforts are intensely personal, written only for the veteran's immediate family and closest comrades. A few, such as E. B. Sledge's *With the Old Breed at Pelelieu and Okinawa* (Novato, CA: Presidio Press, 1981), have become classics. Others are of enduring value for today's military professionals, as they illuminate important lessons about leadership, training, combat motivation, and other timeless topics for those who will face them on future battlefields. As the World War II generation passes from the scene, the supply of such accounts will inevitably diminish.

The air war produced a small but significant body of noteworthy aircrew memoirs. Prominent among these are Bert Stiles' *Serenade to the Big Bird* (New York: Norton, 1952), an account of United States Army Air Forces (USAAF) B-17 operations over Germany in 1944; Guy Gibson's *Enemy Coast Ahead* (London: Michael Joseph, 1946), perhaps the best of the Royal Air Force Bomber Command aircrew memoirs; and Alvin Kernan's *Crossing the Line: A Bluejacket's World War II Odyssey* (Annapolis, MD: Naval Institute Press, 1994), offering valuable perspectives on the carrier war in the Pacific from an enlisted man's point of view. Such memoirs capture the drama of aerial combat and the romance of aviation, and broaden and deepen our understanding of the experience of war.

Air-to-Ground Battle for Italy is a recently written personal account that takes its place alongside the well-known works mentioned above. The story of a young fighter pilot from basic training through the end of the war in Europe, this short memoir is a welcome addition to the literature of World War II aviation. It is noteworthy for a number of reasons. It illuminates the world of tactical aviation, which has taken a backseat to stories of strategic bombing and air superiority combat. It takes place in a theater of war often considered a backwater when compared to the events in Western Europe or the Central Pacific. Perhaps most importantly, it combines the immediacy of contemporary impressions with the reflections possible after a long and distinguished Air Force career.

Michael C. McCarthy was part of the first wave of young Americans who joined up in the aftermath of Pearl Harbor. His peer group, graduates of aviation cadet Class 43-A, arrived at the North African front in the spring of 1943 as part of an enormous bow wave of American human and industrial mobilization. His account of flight training is one of the best available anywhere and captures—in microcosm—the huge undertaking required to produce thousands of highly trained combat crews for the Allied war effort. McCarthy and his comrades joined the veterans of the prewar Army Air Corps who had held the line from El Alamein through the desperate battles around Kasserine Pass. McCarthy spent his entire war with the 57th Fighter Group, first flying the Curtiss P-40 Warhawk and later the powerful Republic P-47 Thunderbolt.

His battlefield was not in the stratosphere over the Third Reich, escorting the massed bomber formations of the Mighty Eighth Air Force. His war began with a ferry flight from Lagos, Nigeria, to Cairo; to Cape Bon, Tunisia, after the Axis defeat in North Africa; through the invasion of Sicily in July 1943 and the long slog up the Italian peninsula in 1943–1944 including landings at Salerno, Anzio, and the battles around Monte Cassino, with a brief detour in support of the invasion of southern France.

While his memoir speaks of plenty of air combat with the Messerschmitt Bf 109s and Focke-Wulf Fw 190s of the Luftwaffe's fighter force, the greatest enemy McCarthy and his comrades faced was German antiaircraft fire. Their unglamorous business was conducting interdiction and close air support, part of a lengthy and costly combined-arms effort to leverage the Germans out of their powerful defensive positions on the Italian peninsula. Most noteworthy of the interdiction campaigns was Operation Strangle (19 March–10 May 1944). The operation's goal was "to reduce the enemy's flow of supplies to a level which will make it impracticable for him to maintain and operate his forces in central Italy."[1] Interdiction, particularly of rail traffic, was normally the specialty of medium and heavy bombers, but for Strangle, units such as McCarthy's 57th Fighter Group and other fighter-bomber units of XII Air Support Command would have a vital role to play as well. The Army Air Forces' official historians observed:

> The decision to employ large numbers of fighter bombers was based upon the principle that the success of STRANGLE would depend upon "simultaneous interdiction," a phrase which meant that, irrespective of whether yards or bridges got top billing, complete interdiction could be achieved only if all lines leading out from the Po Valley were cut simultaneously. It was felt that to accomplish this the work of the mediums must be supplemented by that of fighter-bombers, which could operate on days when weather precluded missions by the mediums, cut stretches of open track, and smash motor transport when the enemy shifted the bulk of his supply from rails to roads. The scheme thus to employ the fighter-bombers was one of the significant experiments of the war in the use of a tactical air force to prepare the way for a large-scale ground offensive.[2]

The results of Operation Strangle are still the subject of vigorous debate.[3] The operation failed to achieve its most ambitious aim—the collapse of German positions in central Italy through air interdiction alone—yet the effect of Allied airpower on German combat power and its ability to resist a subsequent Allied ground offensive is undeniable. McCarthy reminds us what this all meant for those at the sharp end—a P-40 disintegrating in the explosion of an ammunition wagon or a strafing P-47 returning to base after colliding with a 100-foot tall pine tree. He notes starkly, "The air-to-ground environment is brutal, life threatening, and consistently dangerous. Fighter pilot population in our squadron changed 400 percent from May 1943 until the end of the war in June 1945."

McCarthy notes that his combat experience validated the central tenets of Field Manual (FM) 100-20, *Command and Employment of Air Power*. The manual, issued in July 1943 after the early experiences of the Mediterranean campaign, maintained that the missions of the tactical air forces, of which 57th Fighter Group was a part, consist[ed] of three phases of operations in the following order of priority:

(1) First priority.- To gain the necessary degree of air superiority. . .

(2) Second priority.- To prevent the movement of hostile troops and supplies into the theater of operations or within the theater.

(3) Third priority.- To participate in a combined effort of the air and ground forces, in the battle area, to gain objectives on the immediate front of the ground forces.[4]

Air-to-Ground Battle for Italy is, at bottom, the story of how this key Army Air Forces doctrinal concept became reality. Yet, it tells us so much more about the difficult business of preparing for and executing combat operations. McCarthy speaks of the rigors of training, where the washout rate was high. He candidly describes the fear that seized him and his comrades as they prepared to fly in combat—and how some gave into their fears and returned to base with mysterious and nonreproducible mechanical malfunctions. He recounts fatal errors of judgment—his and others'. An example is the accident that occurred after a seasoned flight commander "went to bat" for a talented, yet immature, subordinate. McCarthy believed that the young pilot was still unready for the demanding job of element leader—yet acceded to the flight commander's wishes. The young pilot collided with the wingman of his section leader, killing both of them. "I blame myself for failing to follow my own convictions," McCarthy unflinchingly recalls. "I learned from that experience that responsible leadership demands tough decisions. I should have intervened but I did not."

We are fortunate that Michael C. McCarthy took the trouble to commit his combat experiences to paper. Military professionals and military historians are in his debt. He tells a story that, while rooted firmly in the Air Force's past, is in its essential elements timeless.

Notes

1. Wesley Frank Craven and James Lea Cate, eds., *The Army Air Forces in World War II*, vol. 3, *Europe: Argument to V-E Day, January 1944 to May 1945* (1949; new imprint, Washington, D.C.: Office of Air Force History, 1983), 373.

2. Ibid., 374.

3. Eduard Maximilian Mark, *Aerial Interdiction: Air Power and the Land Battle in Three American Wars* (Washington, D.C.: Center for Air Force History, 1994), 160ff.

4. War Department Field Manual (FM) 100-20, *Command and Employment of Air Power*, 21 July 1943, 10–11.

Chapter 1

Great Adventure Begins

Class 43-A was among the first aviation cadet classes to complete pilot training, graduate as second lieutenants, and head for combat. We had signed up within days after Pearl Harbor.

In Boston, we were the first group exposed to the comprehensive written test designed for those with less than two years of college. Fortunately, Boston Latin School (established 1635), the oldest public school in the country, had prepared me very well. I survived to face batteries of mechanical aptitude and psychological tests and the most thorough physical exams you could imagine. Of the hundreds who began this process, only 41 made it to active duty as aviation cadets.

Our train from Boston arrived in Los Angeles on 23 March 1942. Army trucks took us to Santa Ana Army Air Base, one of many preflight schools springing up all over the country to process the thousands upon thousands needed to crew airplanes coming off production lines at an astounding rate. Santa Ana was a new tent city without roads, buildings, or amenities.

Although the wettest rainy season in memory was underway, our drill sergeants were all business with a marvelous can-do attitude. We were absorbed smoothly into a tough boot camp routine. The testing to identify those who would enter pilot, navigator, or bombardier training was still our major activity every day.

After nine weeks, the process ended. I was among those ordered to primary flight training at Thunderbird One in Glendale, Arizona, northwest of Phoenix. We were pleased to find a mature training facility with excellent buildings, hangars, and roads. There was even a parade ground with carefully manicured grass. An Army major commanded a small, efficient military detachment. His job was to make certain the civilian contractor operated the base, maintained the airplanes, furnished qualified instructors, and produced graduates who met

Army performance standards. Military instructors flew all flight checks to guarantee contractor performance.

This primary school was running smoothly. We were assimilated into a program that split flying and academics into half days. We rotated mornings and afternoons with the upper class every week. The first ride familiarized us with the airplane, area, and traffic pattern and, I suspect, identified those disposed toward airsickness. The instructor did the flying including hard aerobatics. At 20, Roy Martin seemed young to be an instructor. He was excellent and flew with marvelous precision.

As students, we flew an open cockpit biplane from the rear seat both dual and solo. Like many of my generation, I had not been near an airplane before that first ride. Nothing in my past could have prepared me. I adapted readily, seemed to learn quickly, and handled air work—stalls, spins, steep turns, climbs, and descents—satisfactorily. Therefore, I proceeded to the traffic pattern before my classmates.

The rear instrument panel had neither airspeed nor attitude indicator. The needle and ball was the only device on the panel to help with bank angle and direction of turn. We judged airspeed by the sound of the airstream through guy wires holding both wings together. We used wires from the top wing to the fuselage ahead of the front cockpit to judge angle of bank. One wire was set for 30 degrees and another for a 45-degree bank turn. These computations were simple, but I was lost on airspeed until Roy helped me associate certain wind sounds with specific airspeeds. When I made that transition, my patterns stabilized. In a short time, I could land consistently in the right place on airspeed in a three-point attitude.

Later at our auxiliary field after three good landings, Roy had me taxi to the windsock in the center of the landing area. I wondered about this change in the training sequence. With the engine idling, I held the brakes while Roy got out and secured his seatbelt. With a grin, he leaned into my cockpit, said he had seen enough airplane abuse, told me to shoot three full-stop landings, and come back to the windsock.

On the way out for takeoff, I took some deep breaths. Everything settled down when I pushed the throttle to the stop. The airplane responded as if it knew only one guy was in charge. I flew precisely, nailed airspeeds, and wound up on final with the correct glide angle. My touchdown was soft and in the right place. Rolling out, my attention wandered and I could not stop a slow, steady 360-degree turn, the infamous ground loop, a Stearman trait responsible for the failure of hundreds of students throughout that aircraft's long career as the Army's primary trainer. Since neither wingtip touched the ground during my ground loop, I continued the solo, flew the next two patterns, then returned to the windsock where Roy verified no wingtip damage and strapped in. With a terse "I have the airplane," he flew us home without another word. His debriefing combined an essential lesson with a classic "butt chewing" of which there have been several in my long career, but this one was well done. I should have returned to the windsock and let Roy examine the airplane and decide the status of the solo. Otherwise, my performance had been satisfactory. The lesson was to always concentrate on flying the airplane until it is parked safely and chocked.

After the solo, Roy introduced the whole range of aerobatic maneuvers such as snap, slow, and barrel and aileron rolls plus over the top loops, Immelmanns, Cuban eights, and cloverleafs. I needed a hard week of dual rides before I approached the precision in these maneuvers that Roy considered necessary. The airplane demanded a lot of muscle before rewarding its pilot with a well-turned aerobatic sequence.

Eventually, Roy had enough confidence in me to schedule my first check ride, and I passed successfully. The only comment from the Army first lieutenant was a short "nice work." Completion of the transition check let me fly solo without close supervision.

With pressure somewhat reduced, I could pay attention to my classmates. Many had not soloed even though they had the necessary dual rides and flying time. Now they were headed for the "washing machine." Once on that track, most would not beat the system. A few might slip to the next class with another chance to fly, but the majority would become bombardiers or navigators. The pace was demanding, and the pressure intense.

Daytime heat in the Arizona desert left all of us with an energy deficit that would get much worse. Our class, accompanied by one-half of the airplanes, instructors, and support personnel, was ordered to open a new primary school—Thunderbird Two in Scottsdale—now a beautiful, green, well-developed part of Phoenix. In 1942, it was an inhospitable desert where afternoon winds felt like a blowtorch. Temperatures often reached 120 degrees. The move to Scottsdale, a distance of 60 miles, was simple. The ground party included classmates responsible for our baggage. Others flew with an instructor. Some who had completed the transition check flew solo behind an instructor's airplane. I had that pleasant experience.

The new base was hardly ready for occupancy. There were shutters but no glass in the windows so dust was everywhere. A room inspection before breakfast everyday was mandatory and dust was an automatic failure item. Without air conditioning, nighttime temperatures hovered around 100 degrees, so fitful sleep complicated our quality of life especially for those in program trouble.

The attrition rate climbed dramatically. Sheer exhaustion affected that unfortunate statistic. I passed the final flight check early, which meant I would graduate. The focus then was to get everyone through final checks.

The rest of us were flying daily with little supervision. We managed to abuse the privilege. Carefree, a beautiful resort town nestled in foothills south of Flagstaff, was at the northern edge of the flying area. We decided to meet there, buzz the town, and return to base. Surely, those nice folks would tolerate our idea of good clean fun. More than a dozen of us were stupid enough to pull this stunt. We survived to fly again because the Army needed pilots badly. The base commander was on the phone for hours. Carefree residents were furious. The thorough buzz job included low passes, even low-level aerobatics from every direction, all unplanned and certainly not briefed. Only a miracle let us avoid buildings, trees, and each other. After landing, we were isolated. With parachutes on our backs, we walked tours on the ramp in the heat. We would not learn our fate for 48 hours. The base commander did not terminate us. However, we did not fly again at Thunderbird Two.

GREAT ADVENTURE BEGINS

Every dirty job on the base was ours, but there were no complaints. We were thankful to be still in the program.

With relief, we rolled out of the gate headed for Marana about 30 miles northwest of Tucson. Buses took us to the Phoenix train station for the two-hour trip. We stopped in the middle of nowhere, surrounded by sagebrush, with no sign of life. After the train left, we waited in desert silence. Soon, an approaching jeep appeared on the west side of the tracks. A first lieutenant, calling us to attention, welcomed the first class to Marana. He was the base commander. In trucks, we proceeded up the hill to what was another bare base marginally ready for occupancy. The fact that our class had to deal with primitive conditions at Santa Ana, Thunderbird Two, and now, Marana, reflects on the tremendous mobilization capability of our great country. Only now as I remember these events have I come to appreciate how remarkable it was that our Army was able to produce highly qualified aircrews under such tough conditions.

Graduates from two other primary schools joined us in the Arizona desert 30 miles from Tucson. Despite living conditions, the program began smoothly. The BT-13 Vultee "Vibrator" was a low-wing, metal airplane with fixed gear, 450-horsepower engine, complete instrument panels, radios, and sliding canopies. Army personnel staffed Marana. Our instructors had experience in operational squadrons. They were products of the accelerated training system, which began when war clouds loomed over Europe in the late 1930s.

My instructor, Lieutenant Tanner, was a quiet, older man who was an excellent instructor and a gifted pilot. The BT-13 was not difficult to fly. A wide landing gear minimized the ground-loop potential. The airplane had a nice feel, and I adjusted quickly. Lieutenant Tanner moved me through solo, advanced maneuvers, and the proficiency flight check ahead of his other students. Cleared to fly solo without close supervision, I remembered Carefree and obeyed the rules with no deviation.

Although I was scrupulous with regard to duties, two incidents almost ended my flying career. In the Stearman, the quickest, safest traffic pattern entry was to spin down from 1,500 feet above pattern altitude and recover on the 45-degree leg to the downwind at the correct altitude. I used this technique whenever I had a choice in the BT-13. Late one afternoon, I returned from the practice area 2,000 feet above the pattern, checked for traffic, entered my two-turn spin, kicked opposite rudder to recover, and waited for rotation to slow before popping the stick forward. Unexpectedly, the spin accelerated—now I was in trouble—losing altitude with few options. I had to get out. Sliding the canopy back, I opened the seat belt. As I stood up, spin rotation slowed dramatically. I sat down, popped the stick forward, and was out of the spin. Still in trouble with nose pointed straight down, I pulled maximum backpressure without stalling and managed to level off right on the sagebrush.

Needing to settle down and review these scary events, I returned to the practice area. With fuel and time available, I circled comfortably. I had applied spin procedures correctly. What was different about this particular airplane? I was the first student to fly it. Had I missed something in the forms or the cockpit? In the center of the panel in bold red letters on a white background was the warning "DO NOT SPIN THIS AIRPLANE." It was impossible to miss, but I certainly did. After landing, I saw a second "DO NOT SPIN" warning prominently displayed in the aircraft form. How could I have missed either one? Reporting my stupidity, Lieutenant Tanner used this incident as an object lesson for the class. Certain of these airplanes had trouble recovering from spins. A clear entry in the form coupled with a prominent warning in the center of the instrument panel should allow such an aircraft to be flown safely.

The second incident was different. I found myself scheduled for an elimination ride where the odds against survival were very high. In the flight shack, those not on the schedule had to sweep out the flight room, tidy up generally, and do the same in the flight commander's private office. On this particular day all instructors were flying. We two students, not flying, split the workload. I took the flight commander's office, left the door open, cleaned, and dusted. We finished and went back to our studies. When flying ended, the posting of the next day's schedule followed the usual debriefings. In the midst of this routine, the flight commander's door flew open. Lieutenant

Watson called the room to attention and asked those assigned to cleanup to report to his office. We marched in, saluted, and waited at attention while the flight commander finished paperwork of some kind. My cleanup partner was excused. I had worked the office. His questions focused on the class grade sheet. How did it happen to be on top of the desk when it was supposed to be under the blotter away from the prying eyes of students? I had not looked at anything on the desk, nor had I disturbed anything. He did not believe my denial. Lieutenant Watson sent me to march the ramp with my chute until the class finished debriefings.

When I returned, my instructor told me I was scheduled for an elimination ride with Lieutenant Watson. Lieutenant Tanner failed to persuade the flight commander to make a change. The elimination ride was still on. Almost certainly, I was on my way out of the program. I decided to give it my best shot. Before flight, Lieutenant Watson questioned me about every normal and emergency procedure in the book, power settings, airspeeds, and altitudes for all in-flight maneuvers, even procedures to and from the practice areas. It was in that situation, knowing that any mistake would end my flying career, that I learned to concentrate and refused to let fear or pressure degrade my performance. Lieutenant Watson had me demonstrate every maneuver in the syllabus. We were airborne longer than expected. In my mind, failure was certain. I resolved to make the last landing one to remember. It was an absolute grease job. I could not tell when the wheels touched the ground. After we parked, Lieutenant Watson had me continue punishment tours. Two hours later, Lieutenant Tanner met me with the unexpected news that I had survived. Lieutenant Watson was impressed with my performance, especially under the heavy pressure of an elimination ride.

One last comment about this incident, in June 1945 after the war, I was on my way home—a 23-year-old major with 154 combat missions and 27 months in the same fighter squadron. At the officer's club in Naples, Italy, I saw a familiar face in the crowd around the bar. Lieutenant Watson was now a captain. I tapped his shoulder and enjoyed his shocked expression when he recognized me. I chose not to mention Marana, talking instead about my assignments and asked about his war. Captain Watson failed to make it in a fighter unit. He flew the C-47 in a support role during the final year of the war. I resisted the temptation to get even. Captain Watson had kept me in the program when he had the authority and opportunity to wash me out.

There were no more surprises at Marana. Instrument training and formation and night flying were new and different, but I maintained my place in the class. In due course, the end of the basic phase found us waiting for orders to either single- or twin-engine advanced training. I did not know how the selection process worked, but I was among those posted to Luke Field, Arizona, an established base, northwest of Phoenix about five miles beyond Thunderbird One. We would fly the single-engine AT-6, with a powerful 650-horsepower engine, retractable gear, and performance comparable to prewar fighters. It demanded care on landing because of narrow gear. Ground loops would claim washouts in every class. The base had permanent two-story wooden barracks, paved roads, wonderful mess halls, gyms, and base exchanges. We had returned to the real world. Luke accommodated many students. There were more airplanes than we had seen anywhere. Like Marana, our class was combined with graduates of other basic schools. If, indeed, all finished this phase without further attrition, we would number almost 500 brand new second lieutenants on graduation day.

As we moved from one phase to another in pursuit of our wings, the pressure and pace of training increased exponentially. It became clear we would be treated as professional airmen and expected to take responsibility for our own progress. We would not be spoon-fed. If we did not keep up, there would be no second chances. Some of us did just that and were dropped from the program.

As we neared the end of December 1942, we wondered about our next assignment, the next airplane, and whether we would go to Europe or the Pacific. The rundown to the 4 January 1943 graduation date included preparation for the parade that would precede the formal ceremony in the base theater. All cadets would receive gold second lieutenant insignia along with silver wings. My class rank, cadet captain, put me among the top dozen of 400 student pilots. It also meant I would lead one hundred of my classmates in the parade. Since I was a guy who needs a string on one hand to know the difference between left and right, my guys were likely to be out of step with the formation.

I remember two pleasant events during those final weeks. Four cadet officers were told to report to the cafeteria in the base exchange where we met a beautiful young movie starlet who would go on to a magical musical career on screen and television—Dinah Shore. She was pleasant, affable, interested, and aware we would soon be in combat.

In the second instance, the director of pilot training selected me to speak to students at Marana about the advanced program at Luke. A new AT-6 was waiting for my instructor and me at base operations the next morning. Cadets from the senior class met us and escorted us to the base theater where we were introduced. I gave my speech—my first. I do not remember what I said but I had the good sense to keep it brief and to the point. At lunch with their instructors, the conversation was relaxed without the formal stiffness that often existed in such an atmosphere. To be treated like professionals was a privilege we cadets appreciated. Through my career, I made it a point to treat all who fly as equal members of an elite group. I found a payoff in flying safety, morale, and mission accomplishment—if you respect the dignity of others.

Chapter 2

Three Musketeers Times Two

Christmas 1942 was different. We were far from home, involved in a training program to acquire air combat skills. During those days before graduation 4 January 1943, pressure was on Class 43-A to finish this phase. I had completed my final flight checks. Graduation was assured. Now I could concentrate on options to get home to the east coast. According to rumors, we could expect a week off before reporting to the next base. When my name appeared among those who had been assigned to the 337th Fighter Group in Sarasota, Florida, for combat crew training, I knew there would be time to enjoy home cooking and reconnect with old friends before heading south from Boston to Florida.

An unexpected benefit of coming home in uniform was obtaining a driver's license just by showing up at the Division of Motor Vehicles (DMV). My dad did not have a car. Our neighbor, Arthur Murphy, volunteered his 1940 Ford, stick-shift sedan. With me behind the wheel for the first time in my life, we arrived at the DMV doubting the success of this venture, particularly when the chief inspector arrived to administer the driving test. He saw the uniform with wings and gold bars. The test was over when the inspector heard I was headed overseas. I remember his shaking my hand with the comment, "If you can fly an airplane you can sure as h--- drive an automobile." With that, he signed my license.

Sarasota was a new base with the essentials: runways, taxiways, and ramp space, but sparse permanent facilities. On the flight line, I could see about 20 P-40 single-engine fighters plus two familiar AT-6 trainers. Most of us—students, instructors, and maintenance personnel—lived and worked in tents that were adequate, but not like home. My association with the four- or six-man tent was just beginning. In Africa, Sicily, Italy, and Corsica over the next 27 months, I would learn to love the six-man tent despite cold drafts, the pot bellied stove, and total lack of privacy.

Forty of us, in a large tent, listened carefully as one instructor took us through a questionnaire on the airplane to make certain we understood its systems. The next step was a backseat ride in the AT-6 to get a feel for the long nose on approach and landing. Two-seat P-40s were not available, so we would be treated like young eagles, thrown out of the nest to "fly or die."

1st Lt Don Fudge, our instructor, was an experienced fighter pilot who wanted a combat assignment, but a shortage of qualified instructors put him in a rapidly expanding training program. Lieutenant Fudge scheduled me first in the P-40. This was a surprise because my backseat landings were a bit rough. Perhaps my amazing recoveries impressed him. I spent time at the airplane with a crew chief reviewing preflight and postflight procedures. Lieutenant Fudge then explained switches and gauges, their location and function, gave me time to study everything, and tested my memory with a blindfold cockpit check. With these preliminaries out of the way, the crew chief strapped me in, patted me on the back, and wished me luck. When I started the big Allison engine, I was pleased with its smoothness but surprised by the noise from the exhaust stacks that were close to the cockpit on both sides of the airplane. When a pilot was on the runway preparing for takeoff, the long nose blocked the view forward. I picked different visual cues on each side of the runway that served to keep me on centerline. Holding brakes and stick back, I set the power at 30 inches of manifold pressure, checked gauges, released brakes, and pushed power to the stop. The acceleration startled me. In fact, the airplane was climbing rapidly while I was still mentally in the takeoff position. I caught up to this new monster, leveled off, found out how fast it could go, did some aerobatics, and simulated a traffic pattern to the stall with gear and flaps down. The airplane was honest with well-harmonized controls. Returning to Sarasota, the tower cleared me to descend. At 10,000 feet over the field, I raised the nose to 30-degrees pitch, rolled inverted, and pulled the nose straight down. As the airspeed and altimeter spun past 400 miles per hour (mph) and 6,000 feet, I brought the throttle to idle and pulled the stick back with five times the force of gravity to level off at traffic pattern altitude with airspeed still above 300 mph. Following

Lieutenant Fudge's suggestion to fly three low approaches before shooting the full-stop landing, I was rewarded with a decent touchdown at the right place, on speed, and with the correct nose-high attitude. The airplane was stable on rollout with no tendency to stray from centerline despite the narrow landing gear.

Within a few days, Lieutenant Fudge had us checked out. We were ready for the main thrust of the program—to acquire the knowledge and skills to use the P-40 effectively as a weapon system. Before gunnery (air or ground), we had to learn the full spectrum of formation flying. In fact, formation became a way of life for us. We began as wingmen—always on a leader's wing from takeoff to landing until that skill became second nature. The two-ship element was the basic combat unit. We combined two elements into a four-ship maneuvering section. Each of us rotated through those positions until we became proficient then graduated into flying with another four-ship. We learned different en route and attack formation options and began to understand offensive and defensive imperatives—how to maintain formation integrity under attack. We learned to protect our leaders through all phases of a combat operation. This new discipline was not acquired easily. It was hard work, but we learned.

The gunnery phase was the last program element before deployment and would be the most enjoyable. The airplane was a stable gun platform but required close attention on a dive-bombing run. To hit a target, the "ball" had to be centered (perfectly coordinated with no sideslip). At 400 mph, I had barely enough strength in my left leg to hold the "ball" in the center. There was a joke in those days—if a pilot's left leg were twice the size of his right, you were looking at an old P-40 pilot with a lot of time standing on his left rudder during high-speed dive-bombing runs.

As we neared the end of the program, a message arrived requesting earlier deployment of pilots to fill vacancies in fighter units on Cape Bon. We who had finished were no longer on the schedule to make extra missions available for the others. When the first set of orders appeared without my name, I blamed a clerical mistake, but I knew something else was in the offing when I missed the next list. Lieutenant Fudge told me I would be an instructor. I was not a volunteer. When told to fly the weather recce flight the next morning, I realized a decision had been made. Usually an instructor flew the first flight every morning. I took off, flew the prescribed route, reported that weather would not interfere with operations, and started back to land. The advantage of that flight was the opportunity to make a high-speed pass down the runway and pull up vertically into a tight landing pattern. Whether I consciously intended to go beyond the allowable or not, the fact was that I rolled into a high-speed dive at full throttle from 6,000 feet, leveled off right on the deck at 400 mph, pulled straight up at the far end of the runway, rolled out inverted on a very close downwind leg, dropped gear and flaps, and held the tight turn all the way to touchdown right on the end of the runway. The high moisture content in the air that morning allowed me to display obvious vapor trails from both wing tips by holding high "G" forces from pull up to touchdown. Instructors, students, and the group commander had a front row seat. The colonel was unimpressed with his new instructor and made it quite clear in one of the classic "butt chewings" that have punctuated my career. Before that day was done, a new set of orders appeared and mine was the first name on the list.

Near the end of March 1943 at Dale Mabry Field, Tallahassee, we reported to an overseas processing unit with an efficient group of hard-working administrators, doctors, nurses, and supply personnel. They checked records; gave final physicals; and issued uniforms, flying gear, parachutes, boots, sidearms with holsters, ammo, belts, and footlockers for hold baggage that would be shipped separately to our fighter squadrons. No one expected to see the footlockers again. We were wrong. Mine showed up four months later at a field south of Catania in Sicily. This unit also had tailors who adjusted everything to fit quickly and correctly which convinced me that these guys were good. We were told to load enough stuff to last six weeks into two duffel bags, including flying gear—our carry-on baggage. Later we boarded a waiting C-54. The aircraft commander did not disclose the final destination. We learned our intermediate stops would be Miami for customs, a fuel stop in

Trinidad, and a long leg to Belem, Brazil, where we would rest before the nonstop flight across the Atlantic to Ascension Island in the Azores not far from the west coast of Africa.

The C-54 (military version of the DC-4) became operational in early 1942. It was the first four-engine airplane with enough range to move people and equipment across the oceans to the combat theaters. The crew had to be careful with headwinds and weather. In many cases, the destination was the only option. No other runway would be within range if weather should close the primary field.

With radio navigation in its infancy, we had a low-frequency audio system based on two letters of the Morse Code, the "A" (dit-dah) and the "N" (dah-dit). It was possible to align the on-course legs with specific headings to navigate to another airport in instrument conditions. The on-course audio signal—a steady hum—was audible in the earphones. If the pilot strayed off the heading he would begin to hear the "A" or the "N," realize a correction was needed, adjust heading left or right to reacquire the steady hum of the on-course signal. This was only effective when ground stations were located within 200 miles of each other. Of course, the great ocean expanses made that impossible.

Lacking a long-range navigation system, the crew used celestial navigation to pinpoint positions over the ocean. This worked so long as we were clear of clouds and could see the sun, moon, or stars. However, on our flight to Ascension Island, clouds obscured the sky. Without a celestial fix, the crew estimated their course with ground speed and headings based on forecast winds. When time expired, a weak signal from the low-frequency radio station at Ascension Island was detected. The crew read its Morse code identifier, solved the primitive "build/fade" ambiguity problem, and found the only runway within hundreds of miles.

With no maintenance problems, the airplane turned around quickly. Our first stop on the west coast of Africa was Accra, a major airport in the British colony known as the Gold Coast. Although past midnight, the crew intended to fly one more leg. While we refueled, a captain with a clipboard in hand came on board. When he had our attention, he asked if we were P-40 pilots with our flight gear on board. That question aroused our curiosity. It was his job to off-load new P-40s from the decks of freighters docked at the port of Lagos, a few hours east of Accra. His crew of aircraft mechanics would reattach wings to each fuselage, roll the complete airplanes to a nearby airstrip (also on the dock) refuel them, and complete the maintenance checks. The captain would then fly each one to verify operational integrity. These new airplanes were en route to fighter units providing air support for Gen Bernard L. Montgomery in the campaign against the Africa Corps under Gen Erwin Rommel. The captain needed them flown to Cairo. Since we were going to those same units, it was an easy decision for me. About half of us on board answered "yes" to the question, "Wouldn't you prefer to fly your own airplane to Cairo instead of riding in this bucket of bolts?" Soon we were in Army trucks headed east down the coast road to Lagos. A few hours later, we rolled into a well-maintained British Army Post just as skies were beginning to lighten in the east. We were escorted to individual rooms, offered a delicious cup of hot British tea, and told the houseboy would care for the baggage. The last I remember was, "you will be awakened in time to clean up for breakfast."

From the mess hall windows, we could see a freighter tied to the dock. A crane operator was busy carefully lifting detached fuselages and wings from its deck to the dock, where, just as carefully, the captain's troops reassembled these elements into complete P-40s, which they rolled to a parking area alongside the runway where they completed reassembly and preflight preparation.

While we were digesting this scene and the wonderful breakfast, a P-40 landed and parked alongside those ready for flight. Our captain tossed his flight gear on the wing, joined us for coffee, then briefed us on what he expected in the effort to get these airplanes to Cairo. Each of us was issued one new P-40 that had been test flown. To break in the engine, we had to put 10 hours slow time on the airplane before the engine could be exposed to the power surges of an operational mission. A twin-engine A-20 or B-25 would arrive within a few days to lead the first 12 P-40s across equatorial Africa to the Sudan then up the Nile to Cairo.

The captain cleared us to get started. I took him at his word, grabbed my flight gear, found my airplane, and began the preflight. In the midst of this, a crew chief introduced himself and told me the airplane was ready. I asked him to explain slow-time procedures, power settings, and anything unusual I should know before flight. He was knowledgeable. I was eager to learn. He explained that with one exception all P-40s on this freighter were "L" models. Mine was the exception—an "F" with a longer fuselage resulting in slightly better performance in climb and cruise. All were equipped with British Merlin engines rather than the American Allison. Since both were built to the same specifications, there was no difference in cockpit procedures. According to the chief, the Merlin ran rougher but he understood it was tougher, would take more abuse, and last longer before overhaul under combat conditions. With that, he strapped me in the cockpit, and I fired up the P-40F. It was exciting to fly a new airplane. Everything gleamed, and the instrument glass was spotless. I was impressed with this crew chief. He was serious, conscientious, and thorough, qualities I found in the great chiefs with whom I worked in my flying career.

I lifted off on that first flight in the early afternoon. The airplane performed perfectly. I stayed close to the field for two reasons—without a map of any kind, I decided to fly ever widening circles to fix in my mind the landmarks I needed to find my way back to the field, also clouds were building into tropical rain showers which were part of every afternoon in this area below the equator. I managed to put two good hours on the Merlin before rain forced me to land. I had been the first to get off and therefore was out front in the effort to meet the ten-hour goal.

As we finished the postflight inspection, the crew chief assured me the airplane would be ready by first light the next morning. With an early start, I could get three two-hour flights before afternoon rains ended the flying day. True to his word, the crew chief and the airplane were waiting for me. I was airborne in the absolute stillness of a beautiful African morning. It seemed the whole world was asleep. Only God and I were awake. In my mind, I was on guard. A short meditation on that was quite refreshing. The airplane and I had bonded; we were a team. I took the time to trim it to fly hands off. It responded by holding altitude and heading precisely with feet off the rudders and hands in my lap. I could induce a turn just by leaning left or right in the seat. In the smooth air that early morning with a great running airplane, I thanked the Lord for making it possible. After landing, the crew chief suggested breakfast while he refueled and checked for discrepancies. At the end of the day, I had logged more than eight of the 10 hours. One more flight early the next morning completed the requirement. My airplane was the first of our group to be ready for the next phase.

The arrival of an A-20 late in the day caused quite a stir. I knew instinctively that it was to be the leader of the P-40 formation north and east to Cairo. The fact that it was here meant our departure was imminent. That evening we learned that 12 P-40s and a spare had to be ready to depart the day after tomorrow. Five of us had finished our slow time. Seven had a long day ahead to be ready. We, who had finished, took turns relieving our classmates so they could have lunch. The rain showers held off until the last P-40 finished.

The route to Cairo would be north to Kano, then to Fort Lamy, northeast to El Fasher, east to Khartoum, generally northeast to Wadi Haifa, and finally north to Cairo. Each leg would be 400 to 500 miles or two to three hours depending on winds.

There would be three four-ship sections, each with one experienced "old head" leading three of us "new guys." The three old heads had to fly smoothly and hold a steady position on the A-20 so that we, the new guys, could minimize throttle movements to stay in position. Excess throttle excursions wasted fuel that would be a precious commodity on this trip. I was one of three new guys selected to be the element leader in each section. We, with our wingmen, would take off after the lead element and join up quickly and smoothly in one turn around the field. If we did our job, the A-20 could pick up the destination heading and not waste fuel in a second turn around the field waiting for stragglers. Although each of us had headings, distances, and estimated times to each destination written on our kneepads, we knew the A-20 represented our only chance to survive.

The A-20 took off first and set up a left climbing circle around the field at an airspeed that allowed the P-40s to overtake and join up smoothly. Whether lucky or good, we managed to get all three sections into formation with one circle of the field and headed directly to Kano as briefed. My section leader chose— wisely—to hold a position up sun, a little above a 20-degree angle behind the A-20. This let me pick a spot where I could keep both my leader and the A-20 in sight. With an eyeball on both leaders, I could anticipate variations in heading, airspeed, or altitude making it easier for my wingman to hold position without major power changes.

As I recall, Kano and Fort Lamy were British Army posts literally hacked out of the jungle. The single, narrow, dirt runways reinforced with pierced steel planking were usable in the rainy season with marginal braking action, wet or dry. Therefore, it was wise to touch down in the right place at the correct airspeed to minimize the need for brakes. A cardinal principle I learned early, and still use, is to touch down in the first thousand feet, on speed, in the correct nose-high attitude regardless of runway length. There are three useless components in any pilot's repertoire—the altitude above you, the runway behind you, and the fuel you left behind in the fuel truck. We landed safely in the early afternoon at Kano, refueled quickly, and were on our way to Fort Lamy within the hour. There were no problems on arrival at Fort Lamy but we had to refuel with hand pumps from 55-gallon drums. Since we were short on personnel, each pilot refueled manually over the wing with cryptic guidance from the available crew chiefs. That process was slow. Departure to El Fasher was delayed until the next morning to avoid rain showers that were already building late in the day, as usual, in this part of Africa. It was dark when I finished with the airplane. Our British hosts prepared an excellent meal from Army rations, a minor miracle. We ate with relish and retired early because of the predawn get up time.

We did preflight procedures with flashlights before breakfast so we could depart at first light. The plan for that day was ambitious. Our first leg to El Fasher was a long stretch. Fuel could be a problem. The second leg to Khartoum would also be marginal with a head wind. The narrow runway at Fort Lamy mandated single-ship takeoffs, but everyone slid into position on the A-20 as briefed. Eastbound flying into the morning sun produced stress on the eyes even with sunglasses. I remember being unable to describe the nature of the country below our flight path because my eyes were locked on my leader and the A-20. I was reluctant to even blink from takeoff to landing. Without maps, navigational aids, or viable emergency airfields, formation integrity was critical if we were to survive.

We arrived at El Fasher on schedule, set up a decent traffic pattern, and looked professional as we taxied in and shut down. We had been fortunate to this point, no maintenance problems. Here, at El Fasher, one airplane taxied in with a bald main gear tire. Without a spare, the decision was made to continue and bet on a good landing at Khartoum. As a precaution, that airplane would land last in case the tire blew and blocked the only runway. Pilots were not needed for refueling so we enjoyed lunch, launched in timely fashion, joined up smoothly, and headed east to Khartoum. Now, comfortable in formation, I relaxed enough to bring the terrain into my eye scan. The jungles had given way to less dense forests, the more rolling meadows that characterize the Sudan and East African states. We were over terrain where we could survive a crash landing with an engine failure. I drew a breath of relief as that reality hit home.

When the last fuel check indicated we would make Khartoum easily, our leader in the A-20 decided to put on an arrival show. He positioned a P-40 section on each wing of the A-20 with the third section in trail below the propwash of the A-20. The P-40s were in diamond formation with "number four" in trail behind the section leader. From my position, the spacing was excellent throughout the flyby and the landing pattern. My classmate with the bald tire made a smooth touchdown on the end of the runway and taxied in as if such problems were part of our normal routine. It was a relief to be on a base with qualified maintenance personnel and essential spare parts. Khartoum was a normal stop for delivery of aircraft to combat units supporting the British Eighth Army under General Montgomery. He was driving the German Africa Corps west from Cairo to Cape Bon. American forces had landed in Algeria in

November 1942. They were pushing the Germans east in bitter fighting along the coast to Cape Bon. The trap was well set. It would culminate within days in the defeat of the Africa Corps and force Rommel's withdrawal with heavy casualties from Cape Bon to Sicily. We, all new replacement pilots, would fly our first combat missions on fighter sweeps against German and Italian fighter units over the Mediterranean between Cape Bon and Sicily. We would experience our true baptism of fire when Allied forces began the intense, full-scale, air-to-ground campaign before the 10 July 1943 invasion of Sicily. At the moment, we were about to complete successfully an improbable ferry mission of 12 P-40s from Lagos to Cairo.

After a night's rest, a careful maintenance check, and a final refueling stop at Wadi Haifa, we arrived at Cairo's main airport about mid-afternoon. We delivered our P-40s to an Army Air Corps service group where their combat preparation would be completed. We found our duffel bags at a waiting C-47 and boarded quickly for the short flight to El Kabrit south of Cairo and west of the Suez Canal. There our classmates were completing an operational training program conducted for the 57th Fighter Group by experienced pilots on a break from combat missions. The commander of that detachment, Capt George Fairlamb, had been briefed on our trip from Lagos to Cairo. Maybe that report explained why we late arrivals needed only two good attack missions against abandoned tanks in the open desert to convince Captain Fairlamb to let us travel with our classmates.

Within a few days, the Service Group had airplanes ready for delivery to Cape Bon. We, the last to arrive, found ourselves back in Cairo where our familiar P-40s, now fitted with bomb racks, belly tanks, and ammo, were among the airplanes ready and waiting on the flight line. We were assigned to fly in four-ship sections, each led by an instructor from the detachment at El Kabrit. The 57th Fighter Group fought a remarkable engagement a few days earlier on Palm Sunday, 18 April 1943. Off Cape Bon in the most successful air battle of the African campaign, the group had shot down 75 German aircraft, mostly Ju 52 transports similar to our C-47, but also including Me 109s, Me 110s, and a few Ju 88s and Fw 190 fighters.

The Luftwaffe paid a heavy price in a vain effort to protect the withdrawal of Rommel's forces from Africa to Sicily.

All three squadrons of the 57th Fighter Group were now at Kairouan near Sousse and Sfax on the east coast of Tunisia. The pace of operations had been hectic for months as British forces slowly but steadily won the advantage in brutal tank battles that raged on the African desert through Egypt, Libya, and Tunisia. Our P-40s absorbed heavy damage in the daily air-to-ground missions that contributed to the hard-fought victory. Pilots, maintenance troops, and airplanes needed time to recover. This was an appropriate time to recharge batteries.

During this pause in heavy operations, we flew into Kairouan with sparkling new P-40s and a significant number of newly minted pilots produced by the expanded training program initiated after Pearl Harbor. We arrived in four-ship sections. I was on the leader's wing in the P-40F. Over the radio, the leader hoped rather wistfully that we could hold a decent show formation and not embarrass him on arrival at Kairouan. We came in low on the deck holding steady in beautiful echelon formation. Our smooth leader had planned to pull away from the new guys, but we stuck to him like flypaper. The result was a spectacular four-ship pull up where all of us put gear and flaps down together while inverted on the downwind leg and landed four abreast still in perfect echelon formation, much to the surprise of our leader.

Like many airfields in this part of the world, Kairouan had been open desert until leveled and smoothed for military use. The civil engineers made the landing area a mile square to permit four or more to take off or land abreast. We were met by crew chiefs in open jeeps who led each airplane to dispersed, camouflaged parking spots. Sandbags and slit trenches were available at each parking area. German Ju 88s or He 111s had been bombing and strafing randomly most nights to cause damage and harass our troops. Maj Buck Bilby, commander, 64th Squadron welcomed us, introduced our tent mates, and told us to get settled and meet the squadron at dinner.

The changing of the guard began slowly with our arrival at Kairouan a few days after the Palm Sunday Massacre. Within days, the group had added a dozen new guys to each squadron bringing the group to full strength. Perhaps the commander shuddered at the mixed blessing this represented when he realized that one-third of his combat capability was now in the hands of "Sprogs" as he named his new guys.

The air-to-ground campaign through Egypt, Libya, and Tunisia had been tough on personnel and airplanes. The Luftwaffe could still battle ferociously for control of the airspace which meant the 57th pilots had to fight their way back to base low on fuel and ammo. Several pilots with battle-damaged aircraft had to bail out or crash land on the way home, some more than once. Even though the P-40 was at a disadvantage against the Luftwaffe under those conditions, our guys managed more than their share of victories against Me 109s, Fw 190s, and Me 110s and some became aces, notably George Mobbs, Lyman Middleditch, Rocky Byrne, and Gerry Brandon, to name those I knew personally. Original squadron members could now rotate home as it became clear that the "Sprogs" could get the job done.

My new tent mate, Stovebolt Marcum, was unique. He was one of those pilots who had flown off the aircraft carrier *Ranger*, the only enlisted pilot in the group, and soon to be commissioned as a warrant officer. According to Stovebolt, the only advantage of his commissioning was that he would be a legal member of the officer's club and, by proclamation, a gentleman. With my gear, we arrived at a tent surrounded by sandbags and foxholes. That first night I learned why a total blackout was enforced. After midnight, the drone of a twin-engine Ju 88 flying low and fast awakened us. When we heard him turn around, Stovebolt hit his foxhole telling me to do the same or my career might be quite short. The "bed-check Charlies" continued to visit us sporadically until we moved to Cape Bon.

With the group off operations for a few days, each squadron used the time to learn how well the new guys could handle the aircraft and the environment. The squadrons scheduled us twice in 12-ship formations with different section and element leaders in the afternoon. We tested under conditions close to actual combat. At day's end, our flight commanders would know us. We neither expected nor received any quarter. I flew again in the P-40F on the flight leader's wing. No one else knew about the extra acceleration available in that airplane so my ability to hold position despite a deliberate effort to lose me on takeoff added to a reputation for excellence in formation. We passed the test, and that afternoon the experienced pilots showed us the nuances of battle formations that had evolved during the desert campaign.

After that flight, the group accepted us as "Black Scorpions." Later Maj Buck Bilby introduced our group commander, Col Art Salisbury. Just 26 years old, he was already an outstanding combat leader and would command a fighter wing (two fighter groups) when Allied forces invaded Europe 6 June 1944, to begin the final assault that eventually ended the Nazi atrocity. He laughed easily, had a word for each of us, asked about our families, and seemed genuinely interested in our backgrounds. After the war, Colonel Salisbury and I were stationed together by chance at Air University, Maxwell Air Force Base, Montgomery, Alabama, and at USAF Headquarters, Washington, D.C., although in different areas. Fortunately, this remarkable combat leader asked for me by name when he assumed command of the 20th Tactical Fighter Wing at Wethersfield, England, in 1955 during a crucial period in the Cold War.

Our first missions from Africa in 1943 were fighter sweeps over the Mediterranean between Cape Bon and Sicily. Luftwaffe squadrons were flying far out on the horizon. They stayed several thousand feet higher than we were at 14,000 feet and seldom moved offensively towards our P-40 formations even though they had us outnumbered with a clear altitude advantage. I remember the tension growing as the minutes passed with Me 109s maintaining separation between two formations. Our leader did his best to narrow the altitude difference, but the P-40 was simply out of its element above 15,000 feet. The Germans could begin the dogfight when conditions were favorable. If they could position themselves up sun and well above us, an attack was almost certain. It would begin with one or two of them diving through our 12-ship formation hoping to catch us unaware. They wanted to avoid a turning engagement with the P-40 whose strengths were the ability to dive away from trouble and out turn both German fighters. The Me 109 had a treacherous stall characteristic in a tight left turn. Experienced Luftwaffe pilots could maximize the turning ability of the Me 109 without stalling but they could not out turn a properly flown P-40. We had to be disciplined in the cat-and-mouse game with German formations. If we failed to be vigilant in scanning the sky, the enemy almost certainly would attack from out of the sun. We had to know where they were every moment to time the "break" call (turn hard into them) so we could bring guns to bear and shoot. Although we had many sightings during those early missions and several break calls, there were few opportunities to force the turning dogfight.

One day, a few weeks later, we packed cots and sleeping and musette bags behind the seat, flew the last fighter sweep from Kairouan, and landed on the large lakebed on Cape Bon east of Tunis. The ground party was already on its way from Kairouan with a rag tag convoy of Army vehicles supplemented with captured German and Italian jeeps, staff cars, and trucks. They transported support equipment, tents, trailers, baggage, and supplies with the efficiency gained from moving every two weeks or so as the campaign moved toward Cape Bon from Cairo. This was yet another example of American initiative, creativity, and driving determination to get the job done. The 57th Fighter Group's reputation for "scrounging" and "midnight" requisitioning was notorious.

Cape Bon marked the beginning of a new chapter in the Allied effort to increase pressure on the Germans from every angle. Clearly fighting a defensive battle, they were losing the logistic race with the Americans, South Africans, Australians, Brits, and Canadians. Our tremendous productive potential, not yet realized, meant that Germany could not recover the offensive initiative or the logistic capacity to support an all-out war on three major fronts.

Airplanes were arriving daily on the large lakebed at Cape Bon. Soon we had three Spitfire squadrons from the 51st Fighter Group with Canadians, Americans, and Brits flying together. The 79th and 324th Fighter Groups also arrived. Equipped with P-40s, they had been part of the American offensive from Algeria to Tunisia. Still another P-40 group, the 325th, moved onto an airfield nearby. A significant force was assembling for the next major operation. In a short time, a fourth squadron joined the 324th Group, the 99th Fighter Squadron, manned by the first African-American fighter pilots trained as a unit in Tuskegee, Alabama. As I recall, Lt Col Ben O. Davis, who would quickly become an able combat leader, commanded them.

The squadron living area at Cape Bon was on a hillside east of the airfield in a pleasant grove of trees previously occupied by a Luftwaffe squadron. In their hasty departure, they had left behind personal articles including letters to and from family members. My exposure to the German language at Boston Latin School was good enough to let me translate a few well-written letters between hardworking, honest people much like us. That experience made me realize in a powerful way there are no winners in war. Ordinary people, the most unselfish and often the best and most promising in each country, are those who fight the battles, place themselves in harm's way, and make the supreme sacrifice.

Our daily missions were undergoing some change. The Luftwaffe squadrons were no longer visible on every mission. They were pulling back to airfields in Sicily or Italy closer to their source of supplies, places where they could sustain combat operations during the inevitable Sicilian invasion. Our first exposure to dive-bombing and strafing took place against German antiaircraft gun emplacements on the small island of Pantelleria, perhaps 30 miles off Cape Bon on the direct route to Sicily. The 88-mm guns were dangerous at altitudes where the P-40 was comfortable. The Germans had abandoned that detachment and could not resupply it. Nevertheless, they defended ferociously their gun positions against our dive-bombing attacks until we destroyed those batteries. Within days, the detachment on Pantelleria surrendered to an Allied fighter pilot who, with a laboring engine, had to make a precautionary landing on the airfield.

Those of us from Class 43-A had now integrated into each squadron. Flying missions on a regular basis, our job was simple—be the best wingman on every mission every day. Twelve of us were on the schedule frequently on the same missions. Paul Carll, Bruce Abercrombie, George Blednick, Bill Nuding, Charlie Neese, and Gus Keller were sharp formation pilots. We were comfortable flying together. It was natural to gravitate to the same off-duty pursuits and choose tent mates from among the same group when that opportunity presented itself later in Sicily. Big Bill Nuding and I stood alert several mornings at Cape Bon. We were up with our crew chiefs long before dawn preflighting our two P-40s in case a German Ju 88 decided to drop in unannounced. Bill was an outstanding pilot, but he was an even better mechanic. He had liberated two pristine BMW motorcycles, both of which needed his talents. He managed to get them running before dawn one morning on alert. Things were quiet, no sign of enemy activity. We decided to race around the perimeter road with those two big bikes and were almost back to the airplanes when the scramble siren went off. In the rush to the airplane I got my front and rear wheels caught in two different ruts which flipped me to one side landing hard on my right shoulder. We reached the airplanes at the same time, got them started, and took off with me on Bill's wing. The Ju 88 was unfindable, so we returned to the field. In the 30 minutes we were airborne, my shoulder stiffened so much I could not use my right arm. Bill flew my wing. I landed with my left hand on the stick, switching awkwardly from stick to throttle but managed to arrive safely. Our flight surgeon, Capt Risley Haines, recovering from a late night, dismissed the injury as an effort to avoid the next mission. Fortunately, I regained the use of my shoulder quickly but that was the last time I put myself in the seat of any motorcycle. That painful shoulder dislocation healed without medical attention, thanks to Dr. Haines. I played championship quality handball for years after the war without pain but the indentation in the shoulder is obvious to this day.

    The fighter sweeps from Cape Bon did not produce a turning dogfight or a real opportunity to claim a victory for either side. Bill Nuding, flying wing for Rocky Bryne, was involved in an incident where with some miraculous shooting at extreme range, he shot down an Royal Air Force (RAF) Spitfire mistaken for an Me 109. The Spitfires were on the deck over the water heading west. Rocky Byrne's section, at 14,000 feet heading east, identified the Spit formation as Me 109s. They rolled in on the attack but could not close to shooting range after leveling out on the deck. Bill had the fastest of the four P-40s, so Rocky cleared him to chase and shoot. He could not close the gap and was still out of range but decided to shoot anyway. His long burst hit the Spitfire with disastrous and fatal results. Investigation of the unfortunate incident absolved Bill, questioned Rocky's leadership decision, but did not assign any criminal negligence. It certainly strained the healthy relations we had enjoyed with our RAF friends.

The 57th Fighter Group established a very wise command philosophy that required proven ability in combat, not rank nor time in the unit, be the basis for selection of element, section, flight, or squadron leaders. We followed that policy without exception during my 27 months with the group. In some cases, a captain or major, newly assigned, might fly a complete tour as a wingman and fail every chance to lead an element or a section. It was odd to see a squadron of 16 ships led successfully by a young first lieutenant with a field grade officer riding his wing but the policy saved lives, put the strongest pilots in lead positions, and produced exceptional combat results.

We were to operate from Cape Bon until the last week in June 1943, then move south to the Causeway, an airfield on the beach west of Tripoli. Our maintenance troops supplemented the service group located there to repair battle damage, change engines and guns, and complete other necessary tasks in a major effort to have all aircraft ready for the Sicilian invasion. Our ground troops with equipment, vehicles, and supplies were scheduled to ship out with the invasion convoy from Tripoli, land in Sicily, travel by road to Pachino, our next airstrip on the southern tip of the island, prepare it for operations and, of course, set up housekeeping for group headquarters and the three squadrons.

Only pilots, crew chiefs, armorers, and airplanes remained at the Causeway. C-47s arrived in adequate numbers to transport maintenance troops to Malta to support flight operations from there until the runway at Pachino became available.

Air-to-Ground Battle for Italy

PHOTO SECTION

Author solo in formation flying a BT-13A Vultee, Marana, Arizona, July 1942

Three Bostonians who were part of the original 41 who traveled from Boston to Santa Ana on 18 March 1942; *left,* Mike McCarthy; *center,* Bob; and Nick; Luke Field, Arizona, November 1942

Mike McCarthy at the new primary base, Thunderbird Two, Scottsdale, Arizona, June 1942

Father and son, Mike McCarthy and Miah McCarthy, Boston, summer 1941

Mike McCarthy, first graduating class, Marana, Arizona, September 1942

New basic school; four from Boston, *kneeling left to right:* Bob Chesney, Bill Crowley; *standing left to right:* Ed Kinchla, Mike McCarthy, and "Pappy" SaBich from Sacramento; Marana Air Base, August 1942

MOVEMENT OF 57th FIGHTER GROUP

AFRICA
1. L.G. 174   16-9-42 / 16-11-42
2. L.G. 172   5-11-42 / 8-11-42
3. L.G. 75   9-11-42 / 11-11-42
4. ★ SIDI AZEIZ   12-11-42 / 13-11-42
5. GAMBUT   13-11-42 / 20-11-42
6. MARTUBA   16-11-42 / 6-12-42
7. BELANDAH   2-12-42 / 9-1-43
8. HAMRAIET   5-1-43 / 19-1-43
   (R) R6045   19-1-43 / 22-2-43
9. ZUARA   23-2-43 / 9-3-43
10. BEN GARDAN   9-3-43 / 20-3-43
11. SOLTANE   20-3-43 / 4-4-43
12. HASBUB   4-4-43 / 11-4-43
13. CEKHIRA   11-4-43 / 14-4-43
14. EL DJEM   14-4-43 / 2-4-43
15. HANI   21-4-43 / 6-6-43
16. CAPE BON   6-6-43 / 15-6-43
17. CAUSEWAY   19-6-43 / 13-7-43

MALTA
18. GOZO   13 JULY 43 / 20 JULY 43
19. LUCCA   13 JULY 43 / 20 JULY 43

SICILY
20. PACHINO   20 JULY 43 / 31 JULY 43
21. SCORDIA   31 JULY 43 / 8 SEPT 43

ITALY
22. ROCCO BERNARDO 18-9-43 / 25-9-43
23. GOIA   25-9-43 / 2-10-43
24. FOGGIA 8   2-10-43 / 6-10-43
25. FOGGIA 1   6-10-43 / 22-10-43
26. AMENDOLA   22-10-43 / 16-1-44
27. ARCOLA   16-1-44 / 2-3-44

CORSICA
28. ALTO   24-3-44 / 17-9-44

ITALY
29. OMBRONE   17-9-44 / 25-9-44
30. GROSSETTO MAIN   25-9-44 / 28-4-45
31. VILLA FRANCA   28-4-45 / 5-5-45   *LAST SORTIE*

★ PALM SUNDAY MASSACRE 18 APRIL 1943

First P-47 Razor Back at Amendola, Italy, near Foggia, October 1943

Three of six class and tent mates: *left to right:* Gus Keller, Bruce Abercrombie, and Paul Carll; Amendola, October 1943. First Coke in months! Most photos in this collection were the work of Bruce Abercrombie; *center above*

On the town; *left to right:* Lou Frank, Gene Kowalski, Gus Keller, Jim Novy, Mike McCarthy, Bill Nuding, Buck Bilby, Ed Fletcher, Moe Raskin, and Rocky Byrne; Valletta, Malta, late June or early July 1943

Left, George Blednick and Mike McCarthy shortly before leaving for Malta and the invasion of Sicily; near Tripoli, Africa, June 1943

Playing Pinochle while waiting, three tent mates from Class 43-A; *left to right:* Gus Keller, Mike McCarthy, and Moe Raskin. Photo made shortly before Moe was lost at Ancona, Italy. Amendola, October 1943

Ed Liebing flying number 10 and Mike McCarthy flying number 19, probably Sicily, July 1943

Happy day! Day off, first shower in months and clean uniforms, Mike McCarthy, Amendola, October 1943

Award of the Distinguished Flying Cross, Mike McCarthy, Corsica, May 1944

Pre-mission photo op, Mike McCarthy, Grosseto, Italy, late 1944 or early 1945

64th Squadron commander, *left,* Bob Barnum; and 64th Squadron operations officer, Mike McCarthy; Grosseto, late 1944

Author's P-47D-30, number 31, Grosseto, March 1945. This photo was taken by Capt Fred Ryan, engineering officer, 64th Squadron

Miah McCarthy, sergeant in the US Army, volunteer World War I, served, wounded, in France. My Dad!

Mike McCarthy, just before invasion of Sicily, probably "Causeway" west of Tripoli, July 1943

My P-47 crew chief Sgt Santamaria on the wing of the *Maggie Hogan,* Grosseto, September 1944

Author's P-47, the *Maggie Hogan,* and the group B-25 in the background, Grosseto, September 1944

Author and first P-40 crew chief, Buck Denneler, Atlanta reunion, 1992

Fastest P-47 in the squadron—high speed peeled the red nose paint job! Grosetto, September 1944

Ready to start engines, author's second airplane, dive-bombing with two 250-lb bombs centerline; Foggia, October 1943

Left, George Berglund and E. R. Brown, first Coke! Italy, 1943–1944

Group photo of surviving members of 64th Squadron Black Scorpions at a reunion in San Antonio between 1992–1995 before losses accelerated due to age and failing health. Included are both officers and enlisted personnel—pilots, crew chiefs, armament guys, line chiefs, administrative personnel, and refuelers. My crew chief, *third from the right, bottom row,* Buck Dennler is holding a plaque. *Second row from the bottom, third from left and second from right* are the Fox brothers, both line chiefs. They stayed with 64th Squadron until the war ended. *Far right, second row from bottom,* 64th pilot Chuck Sawicki. *Left end, third row,* Paul Carll, my tent and classmate. *Left end, fourth row* George Wilson, another tent mate. *Third row from top, first three from left* are Bob Barnum, Art Exon, and George Berglund; *numbers five and six* are Bruce Abercrombie, and Mike McCarthy. *Second row from top, fourth from right* is George Mobbs, one of our aces with victories during the tough air-to-ground battles against the Africa Corps and General Rommel.

Chapter 3

Air-to-Ground Battle for Italy

The invasion of Sicily began 10 July 1943. It was the first coordinated offensive action by Allied forces since the Africa Corps withdrew in defeat from Cape Bon six weeks earlier. This invasion marked the beginning of the Italian campaign.

Gen Bernard L. Montgomery, commanding the British Eighth Army, planned to move up the east coast through Catania past Mount Etna driving German forces into the straits of Messina. American Gen George S. Patton Jr., responsible for the British flank and the west half of Sicily, had a longer march, rougher terrain, and a more difficult task. His route was through Palermo on the northwest corner of this triangular-shaped island, then east along the northern coast, forcing the Germans to retreat until they too reached Messina Straits. The British general was conservative, had a tremendous ego, had little respect for the American's aggressive tactics, and did not expect him to be in position to reach Messina before the British would get through Catania, but that happened. This added further consternation to an already strained relationship between two super egos.

The German supply line extended from the fatherland through Bavaria, Brenner Pass, the Po Valley, the entire Italian peninsula, then across Messina Straits into Sicily. Fighting on three fronts, Germany could barely provide the logistic support needed for one. It was virtually impossible to bring supplies by ship through the Allied naval gauntlet in the Mediterranean Sea, so the most feasible route was by rail or road down the spine of Italy.

The Allies knew how vulnerable German supply lines were to air attack. For the next two years, our principal targets would be roads, bridges, rail lines, marshalling yards, and everything that rolled on them. We would not ignore airfields, ports, or shipping, but the most lucrative targets would be found on roads and railroads. The Germans were smart and tenacious, took advantage of terrain, used antiaircraft weapons with maximum effect, and gave ground only when it could not be avoided.

Our three squadrons flew to Malta from the African coast three days after the invasion and began operating from that historic island in support of the Eighth Army until 20 July when the 57th ground party reached Pachino, our next airstrip, located on the southern tip of Sicily. We began operations the next day. The only runway wide enough for two-ship takeoffs was 5,000 feet long and covered with pierced steel planking (PSP) to allow flying to continue in muddy conditions although braking on PSP was marginal, wet or dry.

The front lines were fluid—positions frequently changed. We had many targets of opportunity, including shipping traffic in the harbor at Catania. With Pachino close to the action, we could turn around with fuel, ammo, and bombs within an hour. However, we were plagued until the end of the war by German antiaircraft batteries that concentrated fire with exceptional accuracy. We took hits on every mission. Even our group commander, Col Art Salisbury, leading a dive-bombing mission against marshalling yards in Catania, took an 88-mm shell in his engine and bailed out over friendly territory. He was recovered with minor injuries.

Messina Straits was both the German escape route from Sicily to Italy as well as their supply route. They massed a tremendous number of 88-mm guns, dangerous at our best altitudes between 8,000–15,000 feet. An array of 40- and 20-mm guns, deadly below 8,000 feet, made the combination an effective defense system. Our most important targets, flat-bottomed boats and barges, brought troops, tanks, trucks, and heavy equipment through the straits.

I was now Maj Buck Bilby's wingman. This day we had already flown two dive-bombing missions against shipping in the straits through flak so heavy we were diving through black clouds with vivid red centers as shells exploded. Indicative of how naive I was at that point in the war, I liked my front row seat for the fireworks display. On this third mission, flak was worse. Following Buck with flak bursts surrounding his P-40, I knew why those who pursued this occupation were unlikely to grow old. Dropping our bombs, we continued to the water to minimize exposure to enemy fire. Looking back at the target, I saw direct hits.

As I pulled into formation on Buck's wing, his airplane trailed white smoke indicating a rupture in his coolant system. Liquid-cooled engines overheat quickly and seize without an intact radiator. I called Buck to suggest we stay high enough for him to bail out. His engine seized promptly. Setting up a glide, Buck got out with a good chute at 3,000 feet. We were over water south of the busy shipping channel between Sicily and Italy. I followed the chute to the water and circled while Buck inflated and crawled into his dingy. My element leader told me to stay until relieved. A RAF "Duck Butt" (rescue biplane) was on the way and a fresh P-40 element would replace me. Meanwhile, the Germans had a boat underway to capture Major Bilby. Having plenty of ammo, I destroyed the heavily armed boat. It was listing with no sign of life or power on my last pass overhead. Fuel was getting low, but I stayed until the rescue amphibian and the P-40s arrived. Both showed up within minutes of each other. I left when they found Buck's dingy. He was safe and my part of the job was finished.

After landing, it was clear my airplane could easily have been in Messina Straits. Flak damage was everywhere. My crew chief shook his head at the extent of the repair job. Major Bilby suffered from hypothermia. The solution for him was rest and recuperation prescribed by the flight surgeon effective immediately.

In a few days, the front lines stabilized further north. The plain southwest of Catania was now available, offering bases closer to better targets. We would be able to spend more time behind enemy lines and cause more damage. As soon as the engineers had a runway, taxiways, and parking areas operational, the 57th Fighter Group moved to Scordia where we would operate for several weeks before moving to the boot of Italy to continue our pursuit of the German Army.

We had plenty of space in this piece of farmland but no usable buildings. We set everything in tents including cover for our maintenance guys to work on airplanes out of the weather. We pilots shared four- or six-man tents. In fact, everything including the mess hall, kitchen, and administrative space was housed in a tent. Four of us who had been together at Luke Field and Sarasota, Paul Carll, George Blednick, Bruce Abercrombie, and I, jumped at the chance to share a tent. When a six-man tent became available at Amendola in the Foggia area of Italy, we added two more guys from Class 43-A—Moe Raskin and Gus Keller.

The final mission over Messina Straits completed Major Bilby's tour. He had been in combat since Cairo. His performance had been steady and his leadership exemplary. After the war, Lieutenant Colonel Bilby, on the faculty of the Air Command and Staff School at Maxwell Air Force Base, was killed in a T-33 accident.

Capt Art Exon became the next squadron commander, moving up from the operations job. He was the first new pilot to be assigned when he arrived in Africa at the end of 1942.

The complexion of our squadron was now different than at the end of the African campaign. Those who flew from the aircraft carrier *Ranger* in July 1942 and who had chased General Rommel's Africa Corps from Cairo to Tunis had finished their missions. Replaced by us new guys, the first graduates of the post-Pearl Harbor expanded training program, the old guys returned home for rest and reassignment. Many of them brought valuable combat experience to another theater of operations in a new airplane. Others added their unique knowledge and skills to our understaffed training system.

The effectiveness of enemy antiaircraft fire meant aircraft damage was probable every time we attacked ground targets. This demanded a mindset that was not easy to acquire, especially when we knew of no way to minimize exposure except by avoiding the mission. This desire for avoidance was a natural survival instinct.

Field grade officers from group headquarters were divided among the squadrons to fly. One day at Pachino shortly after the invasion, a major in this category led a four-ship, dive-bombing mission against German shipping in Catania harbor. I was the major's wingman. He flew smoothly and I enjoyed flying his wing. The targets, important flak batteries, were aggressive and accurate. Their shells burst at our altitude while we were still too far out to roll in on the steep dive that would enable us to hit our targets. Instead of driving in to that point, the major rolled in early in a shallow dive. Consequently, he released his bomb too far out. We may have killed some fish, but we certainly did not damage the target. The major avoided heavy fire, but in his heart, he knew we wasted an excellent chance. The major's failure was the reason why selection of combat leaders based on performance rather than the accident of higher rank became group policy.

The air-to-ground environment is brutal, life threatening, and consistently dangerous. Fighter pilot population in our squadron changed 400 percent from May 1943 until the end of the war in June 1945. We lost airplanes and pilots on a regular basis. We changed tactics, varied approaches and routes to targets, and emphasized surprise at every opportunity. In the end, we learned that you must fly down the enemy's gun barrel to destroy the target.

On every bomb run or rocket attack during my 154 missions, I fired my six guns on the P-40 or the eight guns on the P-47 at the bad guys. At least that might keep some heads down, disrupt concentration, and possibly reduce their numbers. Hitting anything was a bonus. I felt better knowing I had done everything possible.

Fear was a reality. In our hearts and minds, we had to find a way to manage it. That way would be unique for each pilot. Not one of us was immune. The major from our group had failed to find a way to deal with our personal problem. In another example, a classmate found his terror early in those tough missions against Messina Straits. He reported a rough engine on the climb to bombing altitude. The flight leader sent one of us with him back to base. Maintenance found nothing wrong with his engine. One of us test-flew his airplane over the field through all altitudes trouble-free. On his next mission, my classmate panicked, left the formation, and returned to base without permission or a radio call. He made a bad landing, bounced, lost directional control, ran off the runway, and flipped over. Fortunately, there was no fire and we pulled him clear without injury. His problem was obvious, but no one could help this excellent pilot find his way to control his fear.

He flew a few more missions but was never reliable or effective and had to be reassigned.

This failure was not confined to my classmate. Supervisors, commanders, and flight surgeons shared responsibility to be alert, recognize symptoms, work the problem, find a solution, and counsel the pilot before the situation grew out of control. Unfortunately, the idea of a team approach to understand and resolve such personal difficulties was still far in the future.

Within days, I had an engine malfunction on a mission where circumstances pointed to the possibility I had succumbed to fear. On climb out, my engine became rough at 5,500 feet and got worse until it quit at almost 7,000 feet. The flight leader put someone with me in case I had to ditch or bail out. Descending through 5,000 feet, I reset throttle to idle hoping to restart. The engine came to life accelerating normally. On the ground, my crew chief and the engine specialist followed troubleshooting procedures but could not explain the incident. The aberration occurred again on the next mission. This time the engine did not revive until I passed through 4,000 feet. I could tell from the skeptical looks of those on the ground that they thought that I was the problem. I suggested to the engine specialist that we leave my chute behind and fly with him sitting in the seat and me on his lap. We would fly the profile and see whether the engine would repeat its behavior. He agreed, motivated in part by the chance to get a P-40 ride. We climbed normally over the field through 5,000 feet. The engine then got rough, getting worse as we climbed until it quit at 6,500 feet. I had regained power previously and expected to do that again. As we glided silently through 3,500 feet, I was now looking at a power-out landing with two lives needlessly in danger. Thankfully, the engine came to life on final. I dropped gear and flaps and managed a smooth touchdown. The engine specialist was impressed and convinced. Minus test equipment, we could not identify the altitude compensator in the carburetor conclusively but it was the likely culprit. The engine specialist still comes to our reunions. His memory of this event is vivid.

In recalling the events of my 25 months in Africa, Sicily, Italy, and Corsica during this remarkable period in our history I have forgotten much of the detail, but the major highlights have returned with surprising clarity even to the original emotional impact. How did I control fear that became a dominant factor in the daily and nightly tensions of a fighter pilot's life in months of continuous combat? I remember something my mother impressed on me as a young lad. We were a Catholic family. My five sisters and I went to Saint Gregory's elementary school in Dorchester Lower Mills about eight miles south of Boston. My wise mother told me prayer was an essential part of life. She emphasized that I should complete everything under my control before asking God for help. We, in those depression years, had enough to eat but no extras. Nevertheless, Mom sent me to school with black patent leather shoes, white silk knee-length stockings, velvet shorts, a white silk shirt, and curly hair. The two-mile walk to school was through territory dominated by some very tough kids—the Cedar Street gang. Those guys saw me and licked their chops. Protocol required me to fight until I won to continue to school. I had to face this combat situation every day. I learned to pray and fight. Finally, the advantage of quick hands coupled with a good offense enabled me to win most of the battles, and the Cedar Street gang backed off. I learned early that uncontrolled fear always deprived me of my physical and mental assets and doomed excellent performance and any chance of victory. That building block taught me to keep fear in its appropriate place. Later my mother backed off the sissy clothes and that let me blend in with the rest of my classmates at Saint Gregory's.

In preparing for each mission, our crew chiefs would preflight; load bombs, rockets, and ammo for the guns; and place a hot round in the chamber of each gun. They taxied each airplane to a position near the end of the runway and parked them in their correct sequence for takeoff. In summer heat, the P-40 radiator did not tolerate extensive ground operation without overheating. An hour or so would let the glycol temperatures return to normal. After the mission briefing, we would go to our airplanes. My crew chief, Buck Denneler, was always there to strap me into the cockpit after which we would talk about anything to keep my thoughts off the mission. Buck was also from Boston. We became great friends who stayed in that special relationship until Buck passed on a few years ago.

Buck knew I needed private time before the start-engine signal. That quiet period was my chance to meditate. I started the conversation by reminding God that we had completed all preflight items to the best of our abilities. I promised to fly my absolute best and asked Him for His special protection. I understood the most important part of this relationship was that time spent just listening to God. The rosary marked the end of my meditation. Buck seemed to know when God and I were finished. These conversations and meditations have always been and continue to be part of my life since I was that little lad in Dorchester 70-plus years ago. The difference between those who perform at their best under pressure and those who freeze or wilt under the stress is simply the ability to control irrational fear. The way we achieve that is different for each of us. Prayer was always part of my mission preparation and the longer I stayed in combat the more essential the process became for my well-being and ability to perform.

We had been flying missions steadily. The operations officer needed three airplanes flown back from a service group located east of Tripoli on the Mediterranean coast. Paul Carll, George Blednick, and I jumped on the C-47 mail plane with flying gear, sleeping bags, and mosquito netting. After a turbulent ride in the summer heat, we off-loaded at a remote site east of Tripoli where an Army service group did their best to return weary, battle damaged airplanes to operational condition.

Two P-40s were ready with the third promised for the next morning. Transient facilities were not available. We improvised by hanging mosquito nets from the wings of an airplane, setting up our sleeping bags, and spending a cold night in the Sahara desert. We were ready by noon.

George Blednick wanted to go directly north to Sicily—the quickest route but over water all the way. Paul Carll, always prudent, pointed out that we knew nothing about these airplanes. If we flew the coast to Cape Bon and had a problem, we might find an airstrip or land on the beach. I agreed with Paul. George saw the logic. With me leading, we headed west along the African coast to Kairouan then to Cape Bon where we turned northeast on a direct over-water course to Sicily.

Paul's airplane ran a bit rough before leaving the African coast but settled down so we continued. Out of sight of land, George reported his engine losing power steadily. We turned toward a small, uninhabited island, Lampedusa, with a short runway used for a time by the Germans. When George arrived overhead with enough altitude to make the field, I told him to belly land on one side of the runway to give me room to land. The approach was clear of obstructions, and the runway was relatively free of debris. The combination of a decent headwind and a minimum approach speed with a touchdown on the end would let me stop with room to taxi back and pick up George. I accomplished that and set the parking brake with the engine running. George threw my chute away, stepped in behind me, and sat in the seat with me in his lap. I ran the power up to full throttle, released brakes, accelerated, waited until the last second, and raised the gear and nose gently. We cleared the far end with no room to spare. Paul, who had been circling with guns ready in the event any leftover Germans threatened, led us to Scordia. On the deck, we made it with no further difficulty. George and I landed easily, but Paul, without hydraulic pressure, had to pump his gear down, which was a lot of work at the end of a tough day. It was an example of the sad mechanical state of these airplanes.

Our innovative decisions were reviewed and then endorsed, since we got the job done and brought every one home. In fact, I established a deliberate policy during my combat tour to do my best to hit every target and never lose a wingman. I cannot say I hit every target, but everyone with me had an excellent chance to do just that. However, I always brought my wingman home although some, badly shot up, needed tender care to get back.

Like Major Bilby, Capt Art Exon selected his wingmen from among the guys he considered the most reliable, especially when the mission looked tough. The four in our tent were often on his list. We could hang on any wing and knew where we were and how to get back to the base. In addition, each of us established a reputation for reliability—the ability to think under pressure and find a way to get the job done. Because circumstances pushed us into flight situations that required decisive action from each of us, we were the first of the new guys to climb the leadership ladder. By the end of the Sicilian campaign, we found ourselves performing as element or section leaders.

In my case, the original section leader aborted after takeoff on a 12-ship armed reconnaissance mission from Scordia to the Naples area. As the element leader, I took over the section of three. We slid smoothly into the correct en route tactical formation position and handled the turns from one side of the formation to the other without difficulty. South of Naples, the leader took his section down to a lower altitude from where he could see vehicles and trains on the major railroad that ran from Naples to Foggia. The other two sections stayed high to provide cover and search for enemy aircraft. The terrain was rough with coastal mountains and many turns as the roads followed the easier path. After several minutes with no sign of activity, we rounded a low mountain, broke into a wide valley, and there on a straight stretch of track was a long train loaded with flat cars carrying tanks and trucks, as well as heavily loaded freight cars. The double locomotive was moving fast toward the safety of a tunnel at the end of the valley. The leader immediately rolled in with his section and attacked the locomotives with 50-caliber machine guns leaving telltale steam spewing from many holes in both boilers. We rolled in to cut tracks with bombs and managed direct hits ahead and behind this train. Now we had this juicy target trapped, but the Germans had flak batteries hidden in freight cars. As we came in to strafe, the sides of those freight cars collapsed, and a powerful low-altitude arsenal came to life with great intensity. Our third section still had bombs. They knocked out two flak cars while we concentrated on the others. With the train stopped and their flak guns muted, we set about the task of destroying trucks, tanks, fuel, and supplies that were visible on flat cars. We were careful of time and fuel because Scordia was quite a stretch and there were no friendly gas stations along the way.

On my last pass, I shot at a part of the train all of us had overlooked. When I was satisfied with my angle, airspeed, and a steady pipper, I fired a long burst. Then I saw the red cross on a white square, the sign of a hospital train. I knew my aim was perfect on this strafing pass and I had just violated the international code. At that moment, the hospital car erupted in a tremendous explosion that meant the Germans had ammo or explosives instead of patients on board. That explosion took care of all remaining targets.

We arrived back in Scordia, short of fuel, with most of us displaying flak holes. We had inflicted substantial damage on German forces by destroying that particular train loaded with essential supplies. My gun-camera film clearly displayed the cross on the white square, my pipper on dead center, and the resulting magnificent explosion. After that mission, I took a regular turn as section leader and was the first of the new guys to lead the squadron when my flight had its turn to lead the mission. This was near the end of August 1943. We had acquired a certain level of combat experience, had demonstrated reliability, and were fully accepted in the squadron. Perhaps our promotions to first lieutenant effective 21 August 1943 meant we were no longer "flippen" new guys (FNG).

When the German position in Sicily became untenable, their retreat across Messina Straits up the boot of Italy did not provide them with defensible positions until they reached a line from Naples to a point north of Foggia on the Adriatic coast. We moved from Scordia to a strip on the sole of the boot close to the beach where we operated for a week or so before moving again to keep up with the fast-moving front lines as the Germans fought a well-thought-out delaying action. They traveled at night; stayed off roads during the day; and camouflaged tanks, trucks, and gun emplacements.

Except for an occasional major effort, the Luftwaffe was seldom seen. Fully involved with Allied forces operating from Britain, they also had more than they could handle on the Russian front. The growing American threat from England added to their difficulties. The production capacity of American industry coupled with the ability to produce well-trained flight crews meant air superiority would remain with the Allies through the end of the European and Pacific campaigns.

In the last days of the battle for Sicily, there were occasional appearances of the Luftwaffe as they tried to protect their ground forces. It was obvious from the few airplanes in the area that the effort was unlikely to succeed. I was flying Captain Exon's wing on a search and destroy mission north and west of

Mount Etna late one day. We had bombed and strafed a flak battery, several freight cars, and a locomotive with fire in his boiler. As we headed back to Scordia, we ran across a truck laboring up a narrow, twisting, mountain road. He was caught with no place to hide. Captain Exon rolled in then strafed the truck while I covered for him. When the truck exploded, there was no need for me to add to his misery.

We joined up and continued our armed recce of the road north of Mount Etna. I caught a glimpse of two Me 109s diving on us from our left side and pointed them out to Captain Exon. He waited momentarily then called a hard break into them. That disrupted their attack forcing them into a turning battle. The lead Me 109 wanted no part of a P-40 in a dogfight and climbed away. I tried to climb after him but the German's acceleration advantage left me behind. His wingman either missed the signal from his leader or thought he could take care of two P-40s by himself. Captain Exon was able to out turn the German managing to get enough of a lead to knock pieces off his tail. The Me 109 was hit but still flying. He rolled inverted headed for the deck with two P-40s on his tail. In a good position, Captain Exon fired a short burst. His guns jammed. He cleared me to finish the job. I positioned my P-40 behind the German on his right side, fired a burst, and saw pieces fly off the fuselage aft of the cockpit. I moved the pipper forward pressing the trigger again, but my guns did not fire. Both of us were out of ammo. The German was still flying although not likely to get back to his base. I rejoined Captain Exon and we turned back to Scordia, short of fuel, out of ammo, and frustrated. It had been a productive mission even though we could not confirm the Me 109 had gone down. The next day, the Army reported an Me 109 had landed wheels up on the beach northeast of Catania with his tail and fuselage full of holes. With the Wehrmacht out of Sicily and pulling back to better defensive positions and the Italians out of the fight entirely, we were in an operation that changed almost daily.

The Americans landed an amphibious force at Salerno southeast of Naples early in September before the Germans could consolidate their new defensive positions. They reacted with a counterattack. We joined in the heavy Allied air attack against the buildup of German tanks, artillery, and infantry. Our forces repelled this determined German effort. We had excellent targets on the roads leading into the beachhead area as the Germans tried to drive the American amphibious troops into the sea.

Fortunately, the Salerno beachhead succeeded in complicating an already difficult defensive operation for the Germans in Italy. We were flying from strips hastily hacked out of sandy areas near the water on the sole of the "boot." In normal times, these places would be resort areas for the rich and famous. Vacation homes stood behind our airstrip. We used a few of them for housing and the mess hall. We were able to sleep, bathe, and eat in almost civilized conditions again.

The airstrip at Rocco Bernardo lacked prominent side markings. The surface was firm sand that generated clouds of blowing dust whenever we took off. It was difficult to see enough of the runway to verify that it was clear. We shared this strip with an RAF fighter squadron. One Hurricane landed just before a four-ship of ours rolled into position for takeoff. The Hurricane generated a dust cloud on the rollout. Instead of waiting until visibility improved, the leader of our flight with my classmate, Gene Kowalski, on his right wing began the takeoff roll. Within seconds, there was a fireball followed by an explosion. The dust cloud obscured the tragedy. The RAF pilot had pulled off the runway to the right. He parked facing the runway at a safe distance, and shut down his engine. The two P-40s drifted enough to the right in dusty conditions to allow Gene Kowalski, eyes correctly focused on his leader, to smash into the Hurricane, destroying two aircraft and pilots. Oblivious to the P-40s, the RAF pilot was still in his cockpit filling out aircraft forms and never knew what hit him. Kowalski was buried with full military honors near the airstrip where he died. After the war, his body was shipped home to his final resting place. He was our first classmate to make the supreme sacrifice. Others would join him before the war in Europe reached its conclusion in May 1945.

We continued to combine search and destroy missions in support of Allied advances toward the next major German line of defense. German forces continued their withdrawal northward from Messina to the Gustav line, which stretched from a point north of Naples to Termoli on the Adriatic coast northeast of Foggia. We inflicted substantial damage on German tanks, trucks, and artillery as well as the trains and locomotives used to return their forces to the next line of defense. It was hard to believe the Germans could tolerate significant losses of men and equipment without losing combat integrity. This characteristic of the German military machine would be central in their stubborn defense of the Italian high ground between Naples and Rome, a process that lasted from October 1943 until June 1944.

By the end of September 1943, the German withdrawal reached high terrain north of Foggia. Part of the British Eighth Army landed at Bari southeast of Foggia. That action accelerated the German retreat and gave us Foggia with its many airfields. The pace of our operations had been hectic since the Sicilian invasion. We welcomed the opportunity to stay in one place for more than a few days. As it turned out, we would spend the winter in this fertile plain around Foggia at Amendola.

Our airplanes tolerated the high flying rate but not without incurring discrepancies. The repair of nongrounding problems had been postponed, but these problems needed to be fixed. Our lower rate of operational missions allowed maintenance to do that while we caught up on housekeeping and laundry and reclaimed long-separated baggage. Mine had remained on the same truck since we left Africa for Malta. Constantly on the move with limited access to hot water or showers, we discovered that a sponge bath out of a helmet liner was not sufficient.

An Army service group arrived in our area as part of the support structure for Fifteenth Air Force B-17s and B-24s that were arriving as engineers completed airfields and facilities. Those engineers were also winterizing fighter airfields. Foggia would be home for this new bomber force. Fighter units from Britain, Australia, South Africa, Canada, and the United States shared the area. We were delighted to find a shower facility in the service group with unlimited hot water plus a steam room with no time limit. Happiness for the 57th Fighter Group was almost complete. We were issued new winter uniforms, jackets, gloves, flying boots, socks, and long johns. We discarded gladly the clothes we had been living in for so many months.

Changes were on tap. The last of the originals, the group who performed well as wingmen and element and section leaders were finishing their missions as flight commanders, assistant operations officers, and operations officers. It was time for them to transition to the United States, and it was our turn to assume responsibility. Those of us who had been acting as assistant flight commanders were named flight commanders. Paul Carll and I came out on orders as flight commanders. George Blednick and Bruce Abercrombie became assistant flight commanders. Our tent was well represented in the new leadership structure of 64 Squadron, the Black Scorpions.

Although the pace of operations subsided to a rate we could sustain over the long haul, our targets focused on major communication hubs, marshalling yards in major cities, bridges over rivers, and power generating plants. The interdiction effort was designed to destroy the enemy's ability to resupply their forces. Other targets appeared for us. From Foggia it was about a 40-minute flight across the Adriatic Sea to Yugoslavian ports where German freighters were often detected by Allied intelligence.

The approach of winter brought a change in weather patterns over the Italian peninsula. We frequently had persistent rain with low visibility and layers of cloud extending from the ground to 20,000 feet making air-to-ground operations impractical. Lacking a precision instrument recovery system on the ground or in our airplanes, we could not return safely to base. At times weather over the Adriatic coastline was flyable. When Foggia weather permitted, we would attack shipping in Split Harbor or Dubrovnik. Luftwaffe Me 109s and Fw 190s operated from an airfield at Mostar not far from Sarajevo, and fairly close to the Adriatic coast.

I led 12 P-40s (three sections of four) and found a freighter unloading at a dock in Split Harbor. As usual, antiaircraft fire was intense and accurate. I set up the steep dive angle I like from a point directly over the ship, held the nose steady on the stack, fired my six guns, and released my bombs precisely on airspeed. They hit next to the stack followed within seconds by a big explosion. My wingman had a direct hit, and the other two sections scored well. The cargo must have included munitions since there were subsequent explosions. That ship sank where she was tied up to the dock.

The Luftwaffe reacted to these attacks against shipping with combat patrols over the coast well above our operational altitudes of 12–15 thousand feet. We added a four-ship section without bombs as top cover to protect the 12 P-40s with bombs. The next time weather was suitable, my flight had the top-cover task. I led the four clean P-40s. We stayed with our bombing brothers until they had released their bombs. As expected, the Luftwaffe formation of nine stayed high, did not attack, but sent single airplanes in vertical dives through our formation tempting us to chase the decoys. After the P-40s completed their dive-bombing, another single Me 109 dove through us. I signaled my wingman to stay with me. We rolled inverted after the German who hit the deck toward Mostar. My P-40F, faster than that of my wingman, was unable to close to shooting range even with the war boost on the Merlin engine. My wingman lost me. The German was leading me to his airstrip where flak guns would give me a very warm reception. Discretion in this case was the better part of valor. I turned back to the coast, staying on the deck. When I reached the coast, I throttled back to conserve fuel and headed directly for the Manfredonia peninsula beyond which was our landing strip. My wingman, who caught the formation halfway across the Adriatic, landed with them almost 30 minutes before me. He and I had a private discussion about the basic responsibilities of a wingman to his leader. We then reviewed the essence of that with the rest of our flight. The message was simple, "You follow your leader even if he leads you into the fires of h---!"

The Foggia area buildup was similar to the one in Britain in preparation for the invasion of Europe in June 1944. Our new force of bombers became operational. They flew missions against heavily defended oil refineries in Ploesti, Romania, along with those in conjunction with Eighth Air Force missions against targets in Germany. We had been using the Foggia number eight runway while engineers completed a permanent runway at Amendola a few miles south. In preparation for winter, we acquired a six-man tent with an oil stove, an asset we appreciated as colder weather approached. Moe Raskin and Gus Keller from Class 43-A joined us. A Virginian, Gus was quiet with an easy southern accent. Moe, from Sioux City, Iowa, was part of a meatpacking family that survived the depression and prospered in the postwar years. We welcomed both as part of our family—two guys from Pennsylvania and one each from Minnesota, Iowa, Virginia, and Massachusetts.

We moved to Amendola when the engineers finished their work and the persistent rains let up. A squadron project to build an officer's club out of brick and stone with a working fireplace became a popular pastime for everyone. We contracted with an Italian stonemason to provide materials and skilled leadership while we provided labor. I had mixed cement for my Dad and hauled bricks one summer while he built fireplaces and chimneys. It did not take long for me to remember why I chose not to do that kind of work for a living. The club came together quickly. The fireplace had a perfect draft. That building was warm and comfortable throughout a cold, wet winter.

During those bad weather periods, the Germans accelerated their resupply efforts on the roads and railroads. We knew they were busy when bad weather kept us on the ground. Our weather guys worked hard to forecast conditions reliably. This inexact science did not cooperate often, but once in early November we got a break. We briefed an armed recce mission before dawn hoping the Foggia area would clear and stay clear. Our weather recce reported flyable weather within 40 miles of the base and a solid overcast to the north with tops at 10,000 feet. We launched three sections of four P-40s with bombs headed north climbing above the clouds looking for breaks in the overcast as we penetrated deeper into enemy territory. After 30 minutes, we found occasional breaks that revealed the Italian coastline on the Adriatic Sea. Within minutes through a larger hole in the clouds, we recognized the port city of Ancona with its distinctive road and rail complex leading to the dock area. Our timing was fortunate. A train with a double locomotive, heavily loaded flat cars, and many freight cars was moving slowly out of the station south toward the Gustav line. We knew we had surprised the Germans because we attacked without the usual intense 88-mm flak. The lead section cut tracks on both ends precluding further movement of the train.

My section concentrated on the double locomotive, destroying both boilers. The others strafed the freight cars. I followed behind the last element on their right side so we could attack "fresh meat." As I rolled in, the P-40 ahead flying low and fast was about to pass over the freight car he had been strafing when a tremendous explosion erupted. I was just far enough away to avoid the center of the burst but my airplane was blown straight up flipping end over end for what seemed an eternity. I reached relatively smooth air where I regained control. The engine was running and control response was normal. We rejoined out to sea with one of us missing. Moe Raskin had been the P-40 directly over the center of that explosion. The railroad station was between two low hills, 600–800 feet in height. A RAF recce pilot managed to take damage pictures the next morning. The entire area was flattened. Those two hills with the station had disappeared. There was no sign of Moe's P-40 which had probably disintegrated. My airplane was full of holes but I got back to base again with another aircraft that had flown its last mission. I wrote Moe's family in Sioux City, Iowa. Because of wartime security, I did not describe the details of his final mission but talked about his tent mates, our friendship, and the fun we had together.

Late one afternoon in November, the operations officer told me our first four P-47s were on their way. It was my job to choose three of my guys; meet the airplanes; pick the brains of the ferry pilots; and learn what we could about airspeeds, power settings, and other essential information. It was less than two hours before sunset when four P-47s peeled up from the deck to make decent landings on the Amendola runway. Our crew chiefs parked them wingtip-to-wingtip. We jumped up on the wings, leaned in to the cockpits, and watched while the ferry pilots went through their preshutdown checks. We found out what we needed to know. All were in commission with enough fuel for another hour of flight. The ferry pilots monitored the engine starts and we flew the four new airplanes before dark.

This huge airplane weighed seven tons, had a four-bladed propeller, and a 2,000 horsepower Pratt and Whitney R-2800 engine with water injection to boost the maximum thrust another 500 horsepower. It purred like a smooth-running Cadillac. The cockpit was large and comfortable with a logical, well-laid-out instrument panel. Power was impressive as was the acceleration. Top speed in the few minutes I flew at full throttle was close to 450 mph. Reluctantly, I returned to base on the deck, pulled up to a close down wind, and slowed to gear-down speed. With full flaps I slowed to the ferry pilot's recommended approach (over the fence) speed, raised the nose, brought the throttle to idle, and touched down smoothly.

After that checkout, the four of us volunteered to fly top cover in these new airplanes on the first P-40 mission to Yugoslavia the next morning. Operations approved. We made certain the guns were functional and full of ammo. The predawn briefing for that armed recce P-40 mission included four clean P-47s. We were last off the ground since our climb speed allowed us to overtake the P-40s easily. We were guessing at power settings and hazy about the function of some switches. I had asked the ferry pilot about them. His reply was "I did not need them, so don't mess with them." In retrospect, it was a poor decision to fly a combat mission after one short ride in a new airplane. We should have taken the time to verify combat readiness of our new airplanes. Nevertheless, we flew a decent mission, provided effective top cover against an aggressive group of Me 109s, and dispersed them with no disruption to the attacking P-40s. The Germans, surprised by the P-47, were startled to find us closing on them when they climbed away after diving through the P-40 formation. We expected our bullets to hit where we put the pipper, but our guns had not been harmonized. I had a deflection shot within range on one Mc 109 with the pipper where I wanted it. By the time I realized my bullets were hitting wide left and low it was too late. I adjusted the sight picture and hit that German but not enough to bring him down. My element leader was also in position on another Me 109 only to find his bullets off the mark. Both Germans lived to fight another day.

We learned a lesson. From that point on, our armorers did not clear an airplane unless every aspect of its armament system had been checked and verified.

Chapter 4

Operation Strangle

The Italian winter settled in with extended periods when we did not fly because heavy clouds covered the target areas. At times the local weather allowed each squadron to continue the check out of all assigned pilots in the P-47. During this process, the group remained combat-ready with the P-40 while we experimented with tactics for the "Jug." In Britain, the P-47 flew fighter escort missions to bomber targets in Europe but had not yet been tried in the air-to-ground role. While excellent in air combat against German fighters, the P-47 was limited as a long-range escort. On the other hand, the P-51 could stay with the bombers all the way to their targets. We demonstrated in Italy that the P-47 was an almost perfect air-to-ground instrument. It could absorb heavy flak damage and still fly. The big Pratt & Whitney engine was incredibly tough.

I flew one from Italy to Corsica taking 45 minutes with zero oil pressure minus two top cylinders. The engine ran until I pulled the throttle back for landing. That was not a fluke. Paul Carll repeated it later without three top cylinders and zero oil pressure. The secret was not to change the power setting.

The Jug was a great dive-bomber because of excellent stability at all speeds. It was easy to center the ball, trim, and keep the nose on the target. It was a relief not to stand on the left rudder just to keep the airplane from slipping sideways in a dive. This natural stability enhanced an excellent gun platform. Strafing a fast-moving train in the Po Valley later in the war, I hit the locomotive with the cone of my eight guns knocking it completely off the tracks while the rest of the train, minus its locomotive, rolled on with no hesitation.

Our group commander, Col Art Salisbury, remembered the work we were doing with the P-47 when his fighter wing in Britain was getting ready for Operation Overlord in spring 1944. He sent six of his flight commanders, two with each of our squadrons, to fly missions with us to observe how we used the P-47 in in the air-to-ground role during Operation Strangle.

During winter 1943 in Foggia, I learned that I am not indestructible, far from it! All the way through Africa, Malta, Sicily, and now Italy the flight surgeons had us on a daily dose of Atabrine to avoid malaria or minimize its impact. Quinine, the preferred medication, was in short supply. I remember the Sicilian mosquitoes being very aggressive. They could find a hole in any mosquito netting no matter how careful we were. The pace and tension of combat operations, the less than appetizing and unchanging rations (British bully beef, dried eggs, and our own US Army Spam) resulted in my dropping 30 pounds from a weight of 165 pounds. I succumbed to two malaria episodes within a month. The field hospital treated malaria with Quinine, and provided a better diet plus bed rest. Yellow jaundice complicated my recovery and triggered a third round with malaria. The flight surgeon sent me to a newly established Army rest camp on the Isle of Capri along with others who suffered the same afflictions. I was captivated by the wonderful mountaintop hotel, luxurious rooms, unlimited supply of hot water, great food, fresh milk, Coca Colas, fresh bread, eggs, bacon, and steaks. Jaundice may have stolen my appetite in Foggia but Capri and its wonders soon brought it back. The Italian girls were beautiful, friendly, unfortunately heavily chaperoned, and they loved to dance. My high school Latin, French, and German did little to improve communication, but the effort kept everyone amused. Two weeks including Christmas and New Years on beautiful Capri brought me back to health; renewed a zest for life; and let me appreciate the benefits of excellent meals, a great library, and the luxury of lazy days. I promised myself to return to Capri after the war to recapture the magic of that special place. Regrettably, family priorities and demanding military assignments kept that promise in the dream category.

When our health returned to normal, we checked out of the Capri rest center, returned to Capadochino airport in Naples, and caught the C-47 shuttle to Amendola. The squadrons we had come from were just completing the P-47 checkout. Winter weather was still in control during this first week of January 1944.

Operations had been spasmodic while we were away. The Germans still held the high ground from a line north of Naples to the

Adriatic coast at Termoli. Firmly established on Monte Cassino, they retained control of the coastal plain to the Mediterranean. They defended brilliantly the nearly impregnable monastery. The impasse continued. Perhaps the promise of better weather, additional troops, and dedicated air support would make it possible to break the German stranglehold.

We now had too many airplanes. We had a full complement of P-47s plus about 15 P-40s for each squadron would soon arrive at the depot at Capadochino. When the weather broke shortly after the rest camp guys returned to Amendola, the group decided to deliver those 45 P-40s to Naples in one day. I led the 64th Squadron with three sections of four plus one section of three. We joined up smoothly, a section on each side, the fourth in trail behind my lead section. The air was smooth with everyone evenly spaced holding excellent position. We had agreed to make a flyby down the runway if the formation met our own high standards. The leader of the last section, who could see the entire formation, called saying "We look great. Mike, take us down the runway." Our maintenance guys, who take pride in their work, expect us to fly the airplanes properly. When we returned to Amendola our crew chiefs met us and complimented the "good show."

After four months at Amendola, everyone welcomed the news that we would move again. Our ground echelons packed waiting to learn where and when. Within a few days, the convoys departed west toward Naples to Arcola on the northwest slope of Vesuvius where engineers were completing a runway, taxiways, and other facilities. Workers were completing similar facilities for medium bomb groups on the northeast slope of this slumbering volcanic giant. I believe one or two fighter groups also moved to strips around the perimeter of Vesuvius. All were to be part of the air support package for the spring offensive. Air staff planners who selected the slopes of Vesuvius for air bases could not have guessed this volcano was about to have another eruption that would affect our air-to-ground battle for Italy.

The 57th Fighter Group flew from Amendola to Arcola on 16 January 1944, with three squadrons of P-47s. All of us, officers and enlisted, were housed in the nearby village located up the slope above the airfield. Our lodging was a square, two-story building with a courtyard in the center. The rooms faced the outside of the building with a hallway overlooking the courtyard. During the next few weeks, our missions focused on escorting B-25s or A-20s attacking entrenched German defensive positions including the garrison at Monte Cassino and then converting to armed recce looking for movement on roads, railroads, artillery positions, certain bridges, and railroad marshalling yards. The reason for this concentration became clear on 22 January when Allied VI Corps, under the command of US Maj Gen John P. Lucas, landed an amphibious force behind German lines at Anzio. The landing had little opposition. For a time, the road to Rome was open. With 50,000 men and 3,000 vehicles ashore, General Lucas dug in and missed a short window of opportunity to strike inland from the beaches. German opposition built up rapidly. The fierce German resistance stymied the Allied effort to make significant gains for four more months. Backed by massive artillery support, 10 German divisions attacked the beachhead compressing the Allied line with a wedge over a mile deep. A tremendous effort by our fighter and medium bomber units forced the Germans to withdraw after three days on 19 February. In support of the Allied landing force during that battle, we attacked enemy troops, artillery positions, and tanks and faced the usual fierce, accurate antiaircraft fire. In this operation, the P-47 proved its incredible ability to sustain major damage and still fly. We found it to be a far more efficient weapon delivery system against all types of targets than the P-40 or any other fighter aircraft assigned to the air-to-ground role.

Classmate Ed Liebing decided to give his crew chief a ride in the new P-47. Leaving the pilot's chute behind, his crew chief sat in the bucket seat. Ed sat in his lap. Because there was more space in this cockpit than in the P-40, the procedure should have been more comfortable and safer. Ed, one of our best stick and rudder pilots, was careful and thorough but did not see an unmarked cable extending from the top of a mountain to a power plant on the coast south of Vesuvius. We lost the airplane and two lives. That ended the practice of two in a single-seat airplane.

During this period when most of our missions were devoted to attacks against the German effort to drive Allied amphibious forces off the Anzio beaches, we flew four-ship sections rather than the usual 12- or 16-ship formations. It was common to have more than one four-ship section working the area at the same time responding to calls for close support from our troops on the ground.

We could see our own volcano from many miles in the distance. On a clear day, we could identify and use Vesuvius as a homing device from 75 to 150 miles especially if we were flying above 10,000 feet. A little cloud caused by hot gases condensing in the colder air surrounding the volcanic opening often capped the mountain. As the weeks passed, the smoke flume became heavier forcing the distinctive cloud formation to resemble vertically developed cumulus clouds that often accompany thunderstorms. I was fascinated with the rumblings; mini-earthquakes that made me wonder whether this ancient volcano would reassert its ability to influence events in the Italian peninsula. I made it my custom in returning to Arcola to circle Vesuvius with the formation in trail to let everyone see what was evolving day by day. Our weather forecasters were interested in our reports particularly as the indications of volcanic activity became obvious.

We learned that Corsica would be the next site for our operations. Engineers were expediting completion of the airfield plus other support facilities. Corsica would bring the Po Valley as well as all major supply routes from Germany within range for the P-47 and us. Vesuvius, operating on its own timetable, had convinced our headquarters troops that our airplanes on its slopes could become curious artifacts for some future civilization as Pompeii did for our civilization. Accordingly, our advance ground parties were ordered to pack and move to the port of Naples to await sea transport to Bastia on the island of Corsica. In the meantime, we continued to provide air support for the fierce battle against the Germans still entrenched on the high ground. The front lines moved daily but real progress was difficult to measure.

An indication of the importance the German high command placed on preventing Allied forces from breaking out of the box defined by Monte Cassino and Anzio was the appearance in Italy of the famous Yellownose squadron with Fw 190s. They retained a highly experienced group of flight leaders who had survived despite heavy losses, superior numbers, better airplanes, and well-trained US fighter pilots. Their nickname was the Abbeville boys, after their airfield in France. We could tell the difference. These guys were aggressive, flew excellent formation, climbed quickly to attack out of the sun, maintained two-ship integrity, and avoided the turning dogfight unless they had the advantage. I remember turning with one on the opposite side of the tight circle, 90-degree bank, neither gaining on the other. I saw gun flashes from his airplane, thought to myself, no way, but he actually put three shells on my P-47—one in front of the windshield and two more behind the cockpit. That is the lowest percentage shot in a dogfight, requiring the maximum lead and a full 90-degree deflection. I was impressed. We would contend with the Yellownoses over the next three months and take their measure in some memorable encounters.

Like Julius Caesar who found the Ides of March a time of mortal danger, Allied fighter and medium bomber groups arrayed around Vesuvius became victims of a sardonic geologic timetable that picked the Ides of March in 1944 for the next volcanic eruption. For weeks, our maintenance guys worked nights to ensure every airplane was flyable. We were not going to leave one behind when Vesuvius erupted.

We were awakened before dawn on 24 March 1944, with the news that lava, six-feet deep and moving slowly and steadily downhill, had entered our village. We loaded the trucks. I remember watching the lava flow enter the courtyard. It was moving so slowly that we had time to knock the ash off the red-hot coals and light our cigars. The 57th Fighter Group, located on the upwind side, avoided the smoke flume with the hot ashes that damaged B-25s on the east and northeast slopes. Flight controls, ailerons, flaps, elevators, and rudders were made of thin aluminum and were easily punctured by red-hot embers dropping on horizontal surfaces of B-25s parked on that side of Vesuvius. Those airplanes would not fly again without replacement of their control surfaces.

We departed Arcola in four-ship sections with our personal gear in the cockpit and two 500-pound bombs on the wing stations. We were available for close air support (CAS), if needed. Most of us flew armed recce missions looking for road convoys or trains. I found a railroad bridge we destroyed earlier in the month. The Germans had rebuilt it, and it appeared to be operational. We set up the steep dive-bombing pattern that produced the best chance to hit the target and scored two direct hits that knocked the bridge with its new railroad bed into the water. We searched roads for truck movement but found nothing. We rejoined, headed for Corsica, and landed at Alto south of Bastia where the engineers had declared the runway with its PSP surface usable.

Our squadrons made the transition from Arcola without incident. Advanced parties had been in place long enough to set up tents and prepare mess halls, clubs, and maintenance facilities. Since they had been doing this for most of two years, they knew all the short cuts and problem areas. In fact, the 57th Fighter Group had a well-earned reputation as the best scroungers in the theater. If we needed something and could not borrow or buy it, we had a midnight requisitioner who would steal it. Our road convoys were so diverse that it was difficult to identify the national identity of most vehicles. We had more German, Italian, and British rolling stock than American.

We were to be a major player in Operation Strangle, the next big air-to-ground operation in the Italian theater. The plan called for full-scale interdiction of roads, railroads, bridges, marshalling yards, shipping lanes, ports, and airports from the northern Po Valley south through the Appenines, the Arno river cities, and all roads south of Rome used to bring essential supplies to the German army. We would carefully avoid targets near historic sites in Rome, Florence, and Pisa.

Photo recce units worked night and day to find suitable targets for fighter-bomber groups and our medium bombers. We would sustain this concentration of force for as long as necessary to deny the enemy any new supplies from the Fatherland. It was useful to have photo confirmation in advance that targets selected for each day's operations were worth striking. In addition, target photos showed the location of antiaircraft guns and enabled the attacking leader to select a route in and out that would minimize the guns' effectiveness and facilitate the element of surprise. The presence of Luftwaffe squadrons with a new willingness to attack required us to add top cover. The area north of Rome seemed to be where German defenses were concentrated in an effort to get their supply convoys through unscathed.

The commander of the 64th Squadron, Maj Art Exon, was hit on a low-altitude strafing pass. He was too low to bail out and crash-landed his burning P-47 not far from the coast. His wingman saw no sign that Major Exon survived but, fortunately, he escaped the airplane. Enemy troops captured him, and he spent the rest of the war as a prisoner in Germany. Capt Lou Frank, operations officer, moved up to be acting commander of the 64th Squadron.

The last days of March and the month of April 1944 were hectic and fast-paced. There were many heavily defended, though lucrative, targets. We flew several missions a day to destroy German road convoys. Power stations, marshalling yards, and bridges also received close attention. On one mission, leading three sections of four, we destroyed a power plant, a factory, two steam locomotives, an electric-powered locomotive on another train, several loaded freight cars, and found and strafed a motor convoy loaded with troops. We destroyed every target on that particular mission. The group selected me for the award of Distinguished Flying Cross.

On another mission against heavily defended marshalling yards and communications facilities north of Rome, I led the top-cover section of four protecting three sections of four with bombs. A mixed formation of Me 109s and Fw 190s were following high and behind, crossing from one side to the other. I could tell they were ready to play hardball.

Chad Reade, my wingman on this mission, was in the latest group of new guys to join the squadron. I remember he had the light touch of an angel despite the fact that he was a big man well over six feet and strong as a bull. He flew beautifully in formation, kept his wits about him, understood his role as a wingman, and seemed to have eyes in the back of his head. Just as the three sections with bombs were peeling off on their dive-bombing runs, Chad reported one Me 109 diving on the last P-47s as they settled on their attacking run. I picked up the Me 109, rolled inverted, pulled in trail, and closed easily to shooting range while Chad covered me. I held my breath with the pipper steady on the fuselage and fired a long burst. The cone of bullets from my eight guns hit the cockpit and engine. The airplane disintegrated, bursting into several flaming pieces. In a steep vertical dive, I watched the smoking wreckage falling into Lake Bolsena northwest of Rome. With Chad in trail, we converted that dive into a vertical climb back to what had become quite a turning fight. With that extra speed, I caught sight of a single Fw 190 crossing above me. I fired a burst, a low percentage high-angle shot that probably missed. The Germans chose not to stay with 16 P-47s.

We rejoined after the engagement that lasted about five minutes with no losses and four victories. It was always amazing to me how quickly the air battle comes together with airplanes in all sectors of the beautiful, blue sky. In another instant, the enemy disappears without a trace. We regrouped after another significant mission with serious damage inflicted on German resources, both air and ground. Heading back to Corsica, we took turns checking each airplane visually for leaks or airframe damage caused by heavy antiaircraft fire. There were no problem airplanes on this mission.

My section was last to take off and would be last to land. I took normal spacing behind the third section putting my guys in echelon. The smooth air was ideal for close formation flying so we had a nice tight, steady group of four flying perfect formation. We came over the runway at 3,000 feet. At midfield, I rolled smoothly into a 30-degree bank. We held that beautiful echelon formation all the way through the 360-degree turn losing altitude to roll out wings level perfectly lined up on the runway heading. We accomplished that without so much as a minor jiggle. I gave the usual hand signal for landing, pulled up to a close downwind leg, did a victory roll just as I reached gear-down speed, threw gear and flaps out, continued the turn slowing to final over-the-fence speed, and touched down softly at the right place on the correct side of the runway. It is unusual to have a flight go as planned, but from takeoff to landing, this was one of those rare events.

In the face of stubborn German resistance, Operation Strangle began to show positive results. Interdiction of supplies, ammo, food, and other essentials forced the German high command to move their road convoys and trains during daylight hours risking certain air attack from our fighter-bombers—A-20s and B-25s. Targets were plentiful although German defenses continued to be determined, fierce, and effective.

In our squadron, we took advantage of the heavy pace of operations to check out new element, section, and flight leaders. Flying as section leader, I would have a new guy on my wing while monitoring how a new flight leader was performing.

One such flight to that area north of Rome produced a crisis that could easily have resulted in a new guy being lost on his first mission. Second Lieutenant Brown had flown the usual practice missions off the coast of Corsica using rocks visible above the surface as bombing targets. He demonstrated formation skills and handled the airplane well. This mission was an effective dive-bombing attack against marshalling yards followed by armed recce until the flight leader found a train moving in the open along a straight stretch of track. The flight leader deployed his assets to destroy the steam locomotive and cut tracks on both ends of the long train in excellent fashion. I set up my section to strafe freight cars immediately behind the disabled locomotive.

I told my wingman to take enough space, keep me in sight, pick his own freight car, and do some damage. We were taking some light flak, less intense than usual. My wingman stayed much too close to me on the first strafing pass, so close that his bullets flew over the top of my right wing, shooting at the same freight car. I moved him out further so he could concentrate on his own target, put his pipper on dead center, and get some worthwhile results. His spacing was better on the next pass, but he had lined up on the only obstacle within miles, a lone pine tree, perhaps 100 feet tall, without branches. Lieutenant Brown, who never saw that tree, hit it dead center with the hub of his four-bladed propeller which sawed through the pine tree, sprung both wings back, and filled the engine spaces full of wood chips and sawdust. The combination of luck, remarkable resilience of this tough airplane, and the grace of God let Lieutenant Brown stay airborne. Understandably, he was in total panic. I caught sight of the airplane in a slight climb heading north, pulled up on the wing, and surveyed the damage, amazed that any airplane could fly in that condition. I talked calmly on the radio telling my wingman to look at me on his right wing; we would keep climbing; and he should not touch the throttle. I would tell him when to turn left back to Corsica. After a few minutes, Lieutenant Brown did look at me. Now that he realized the airplane was still flying, I told him to turn gently left to a heading that would bring us back to the coast. If the controls responded well enough and the engine continued to run without drastic overheating, I planned to climb high enough to allow a safe bail out over water in case the engine quit. We had alerted the air rescue guys about that possibility.

The collision had crazed Lieutenant Brown's windshield and covered it with oil and debris. I told him that I would navigate back to base. As minutes passed with the damaged airplane still flying, it was likely we would get home, but that raised a question. How do we get this wreck safely on the ground? Over the field at 6,000 feet, I told Lieutenant Brown to drop the gear. Without hydraulic pressure, the main gear fell out of the gear wells and seemed to lock down. I sat on Lieutenant Brown's wing as we descended circling to a position on final where I hoped we could retard his throttle without killing the engine. Fortunately, he was able to do that, and I moved forward where he could fly formation on me since he could not see the runway through his windshield. By watching my wheels approach the runway, Lieutenant Brown could judge his round out to a successful landing after which I went around to fly my own pattern. Lieutenant Brown handled himself with courage and skill but decided his luck was gone. He did not fly another mission and neither did that airplane.

Additional fighter units joined Operation Strangle including France's Lafayette Esquadrille who had brand new P-47s and flew with us from Alto, Corsica. Pressure by Allied air forces was producing results. German defenses around Monte Cassino and

Anzio were cracking. US forces now saw a chance to break out of the beachhead after almost four months since landing 22 January 1944. We expanded our operations to the Po Valley between Bologna, Turin, Milano, and the main railroad line running through its center along the Po River. German supplies had to transit through this rich, fertile, industrialized part of Italy to have any chance to benefit their forces holding the Allies at bay south of Rome. Activity in the Po area was incredible. Marshalling yards in each city were bustling where the Germans assembled trains during daylight hours to travel at high speed during darkness hoping to avoid air attacks.

Promotion to captain on 13 April 1944 was unexpected. Paul Carll, Jim Novy, and I were flight commanders on squadron orders and in line for promotion. Capt Lou Frank, now in command of the squadron, selected Jim Novy to be assistant operations officer. Lou and Jim were tent mates and close friends so that selection was an obvious choice. We three members of Class 43-A were completing one year in the squadron. Approaching 100 missions would qualify us for rotation to the states. Instead, squadron officers asked us to accept a 45-day rest and recuperation back home then return for another combat tour. Jim Novy, Bruce Abercrombie, and I chose that new program, but Paul Carll decided to finish his tour and go home. Jim Novy's promotion came through first. We both returned to the states with new captain's insignia.

We were finding the Luftwaffe in the skies ready to attack our air-to-ground fighter-bombers almost every day. Shortly before the end of April, Paul Carll and I led separate armed recce missions to the area between the Arno River and Rome where enemy air units were most sensitive to our operations. It happened that RAF Spitfires made a low-level attack against the airfield from which Fw 190s and Me 109s were operating, flushing them like hornets from their hive. Angry, looking for revenge, they found Paul and his guys in the midst of their bombing attack against a railroad bridge. Some distance away, I heard Paul's section leaders call out many bandits on the attack. Paul turned into the attacking Germans and told me his location while asking for help. Jettisoning our bombs, we turned immediately to join the fight. In minutes, we saw the swirling dogfight with airplanes turning, diving, and climbing in a scramble that typifies the life and death battle between fighter pilots determined not to be the ones who lose. By the time we reached the area, the Germans had enough of the P-47s. Paul had two Fw 190s to his credit but told me on the radio that they had heavily damaged his airplane. I found him circling with his wingman in the area just vacated by those involved in the dogfight. One 20-mm shell had knocked out his instrument panel leaving him without airspeed, altimeter, compass, or engine performance gauges. The second shell hit his right wing ammo compartment, exploding many 50-caliber bullets, forcing the door from its normal horizontal position to a vertical position, disturbing aerodynamic flow across the wing making the airplane fly in a severe crab. This was another example of a P-47 defying the principles of flight, flyable despite serious airframe damage. After examining the airplane from every angle, I told Paul it was not leaking fluids and had no obvious structural damage other than the right wing and the cockpit area. We decided I would lead back to Corsica with Paul on my wing. Because of the deformed right wing ammo compartment, we needed to identify the airspeed at which the airplane would stall so we could pick a final approach airspeed for landing. At Alto, we circled the field high enough to permit a safe bailout. In the landing configuration, I slowed from 220 mph calling the airspeed in 5 mph increments. The prestall shudder began just below 170 mph so we chose that speed for our final approach. I held 185 mph as we turned to line up on final slowing very smoothly to 170 mph as we crossed the fence. Paul held excellent position, rotated, and touched down nicely with plenty of room to slow to taxi speed on the available runway. One distinguishing characteristic of our performance in the 64th Squadron was the willingness to take care of each other. True leadership is unselfish. When you take risks to care for your people, the attitude is contagious and will always pay dividends far beyond your expectations. The fallout in loyalty, respect, dedication, and esprit de corps contributes to the ability of the unit to get tough jobs done with better results.

Before leaving Alto in a C-47 for Naples en route to the United States, one of our general officers arrived to award many of us the Air Medal and the Distinguished Flying Cross to those who had earned it. All three squadrons assembled in clean rumpled uniforms at attention with an honor guard. The ceremony was impressive.

In Naples, we caught a waiting B-17 for a long flight to Oran. We were processed quickly and boarded a Navy transport for the seven-day voyage to Norfolk, Virginia.

Thirty days on leave at home in Boston enabled a great reunion with family, friends, and my girl, Margaret Hogan. She had joined the Coast Guard Women's Reserve, or SPARS (an acronym taken from the Coast Guard motto "Semper Paratus, Always Ready"), finished her boot camp in Palm Beach, Florida, and was on leave in Boston en route to her first duty assignment in Philadelphia. We postponed wedding plans until after the war because we were both in service and I was returning to the 57th Fighter Group for another combat tour. In Boston, a fourth malaria attack was resolved quickly at the Army base clinic with Quinine. That incident in 1944 was the last time the Sicilian mosquito had its way with this fighter pilot.

Margaret reported to her Coast Guard "ship," one of the nice hotels in downtown Philadelphia. I reported to a personnel-processing center located in a hotel on the boardwalk in Atlantic City where we were assigned to a ship scheduled out of Norfolk, Virginia, for Oran and Naples. Jim Novy, Bruce Abercrombie, and I were on orders to the same troop ship heading back to the squadron. Before leaving Atlantic City, Paul Carll walked in to the lobby with Marian, the hometown girl he wed on his return from Corsica. Paul finished his tour three weeks after we left for the United States. His next assignment was a staff job at Mitchell Field on Long Island. He did not expect another combat tour.

The rest and relaxation in the United States, the excellent food, and enjoyable friends and family had done wonders for my state of mind as well as my physical well-being. I was almost back to my fighting weight of 165 pounds.

Squadron members appreciated our return because a shortage of experienced leaders added new tension to operations in the Po Valley where targets were plentiful and important. German defenses finally broke under heavy pressure around

Monte Cassino and Anzio in the middle of May followed early in June by the Germans pulling back from the Holy City of Rome. It was important to shut off resupply of essential fuel, ammo, and parts to the German army. Offensive pressure by Allied forces pushed the Wehrmacht back to the Appenines north of the Arno River where they could again use high terrain to delay the Allied advance despite our greater numbers, excellent weapons, and air superiority. In this final year, the Germans took advantage of bitterly cold winter weather to prevent the Allies from breaking over the Appenines into the Po Valley. Efforts to dislodge German defenses along the east coast also would not succeed until brutal winter weather of 1944 loosened its hold on the Italian peninsula.

I came back to flying missions with no drop off in efficiency. We had several new guys who demonstrated the ability to learn, showed leadership potential, and had the courage to endure fierce enemy antiaircraft fire whose effectiveness continued to be awesome. I was not surprised that my airplane took heavy damage on my first missions to marshalling yards in Po Valley cities. The Germans were serious about making us pay for the privilege. My reaction to facing lethal antiaircraft fire again startled me. I found my system for dealing with personal fear during my first year in combat needed some "tinkering" to be effective during this last year. The fact that I chose to come back to this dangerous occupation led me to wonder whether God was ready to continue His role in keeping me safe. I finally realized God was very good at His job. He did not need my help. When I left everything in His hands, quit worrying, and slept soundly, I regained my ability to control fear.

The Normandy landings on D-Day, 6 June 1944, gave Allied forces a foothold on the European continent that they would not relinquish. Coupled with Russian pressure on the Eastern front, the southern France landing, "Operation Anvil," 15 August 1944, tightened the noose on the Fatherland. The 57th Fighter Group joined the Lafayette Esquadrille among other fighter units on Corsica in supporting the southern France invasion.

I led the first of four sections of four P-47s on a night takeoff from Alto timed to arrive in the target area 30 minutes before dawn. I had as my target the road and rail complex near

Aix, a town northeast of Marseille, where there were a supply depot and German troops. The railroad marshalling yard was busy with trains preparing to depart. I identified the supply depot from a target photo as we approached from the south. We caught antiaircraft defenders napping so we rolled in on an ideal dive-bombing run. We put eight 500-pound bombs directly on the target destroying it.

Off the bomb run, I had seen a long train moving out of the marshalling yard. I told Chad Reade, my wingman, to take spacing. We would hit the train with two or three strafing passes. I stopped the double locomotive on our first pass and continued around for another. Until now, the Germans had not subjected us to defensive fire. There was a dry riverbed south of the track leading out of town. I was low and very fast, just lining up my firing pass when I saw a huge barn door moving away from a gun emplacement hidden in the riverbed. As I passed directly over that spot, a 40-mm gun fired several rounds, one of which hit my airplane somewhere behind the cockpit. I felt the airplane shudder; the cockpit filled with smoke. As I rolled the canopy back, the smoke cleared. Chad pulled up on my wing, told me there was a large hole over the supercharger on the fuselage, forward of the tail. He could see daylight from one side to the other. When hit, I was about to stand up to bail out but realized I was much too low. The engine was still running. Chad saw no more smoke so the fire was out. We decided to turn gingerly back to Corsica in a gentle climb. We suspected the gunfire had damaged the control cables for rudder and elevators in that area. In fact, only one each elevator and rudder cable continued to function. Still in one piece, the airplane was flyable. To get it home would require a very gentle touch on the controls. Once again, we alerted the air rescue guys to the possibility of a bail out rather than a safe landing with this new but badly damaged P-47. We decided not to increase airspeed in the descent because the now fragile tail section might separate from the fuselage. Chad told me later there was no sign of structural support that he could identify from his examination of the damaged area. When I put the gear handle in the down position, the main gear fell out and locked but the tail wheel remained up and locked. Hydraulic fluid from lines in the area of the supercharger had caused the fire and smoke. We let the others land, then, with Chad on my wing, we came around for a smooth no-flap touchdown. I held the tail off the runway as long as possible. When it finally dropped, the fuselage buckled at the point where the 40-mm projectile hit the airplane. Chad's comment about no visible means of support was accurate. This airplane had flown for the last time. Although the P-47's structural integrity survived another test, I believe God cushioned that airplane in the palm of His hand to get us home safely.

The invasion of southern France made German defensive positions along the Rhine river untenable, forcing them to retreat northward to avoid being cut off by Allied armies advancing broadly from west to east through France and the low countries. Air support by our fighter units based in Corsica now required a long haul rendering the effort impractical, so we returned to the battle for Italy. In fact, most of our missions against targets in the Po Valley required a much longer haul than we preferred while we were operating from Corsica.

Engineers were preparing the airfield in Grosseto for the 57th Fighter Group. Allied air attacks had heavily damaged the airfield while the Luftwaffe occupied it. We completed the move to Grosseto in two steps, first, to Ombrone, a secondary airport further inland from Grosseto, on 17 September then to Grosseto on 25 September 1944. The 57th Fighter Group operated from Grosseto through winter 1944 and the first four months of 1945. A few miles away on the beach at Marina Di Grosseto all three squadrons occupied beachfront properties where we established our clubs and squadron headquarters. For the first time since Vesuvius, we were not going to live in tents. Changes in the command structure within the 64th Squadron were in process. Maj Bob Barnum, an original Black Scorpion, who had flown a P-40 off the aircraft carrier *Ranger* across Africa to Cairo, was returning to replace Capt Lou Frank as commander. Jim Novy had lost some enthusiasm for the operations job and the pressure to put himself on the mission schedule was beginning to wear thin. As his assistant, I ran the shop, dealt with the flight commanders, scheduled myself regularly on missions to represent the command section, and flew with Major Barnum to acquaint him with the airplane as well as changes since his first tour. Barney and I hit it off from the first day. He made me his operations officer and the relationship became stronger every day through the final months of the war in Europe.

Summer 1944 brought much change in personnel. Our six-man tent began at Amendola in October 1943 with Paul Carll, Gus Keller, Bruce Abercrombie, George Blednick, Moe Raskin, and Mike McCarthy. Of that group, Abercrombie and McCarthy were back for second tours. Carll and Blednick returned to the states. Moe Raskin was lost in the massive train explosion at Ancona in October 1943. The population of our tent in Corsica before the move to Grosseto included three 43-A originals, Keller, Abercrombie, and McCarthy plus our flight surgeon, Lester A. "Doc" Wall and George Wilson who had joined us at Amendola in January 1944. We had one spot open, but the move to Marina Di Grosseto made that a moot point. Doc Wall was a great asset to the flying community with a wonderful sense of humor. More importantly, he understood the need to know each of us who were under the pressure of daily combat missions. Doc, Barney, the flight commanders, and I met often to discuss how to track and help those who were showing signs of combat fatigue. We used a team approach, a concept far ahead of its time, in finding ways to keep pilots healthy under stressful flying conditions.

The airfield at Grosseto had been home to several Luftwaffe units during the past two years. Many damaged hulks, which would never fly again, were silent witnesses to its operational history. Ju 88s, He 111s, Fw 190s, and Me 109s were scattered around the airfield. One of our crew chiefs met me after a test flight on a P-47 shortly after our arrival. On the way back to operations, he showed me a B-25 which had landed with a single engine functioning and had been abandoned or forgotten by its squadron. The airplane was in nearly perfect flying condition needing only an engine change and a test hop to be operational. Apparently, a new engine was on order and had just arrived along with P-47 engines for the 57th Fighter Group. This crew chief had worked on B-25s before he left the states, was familiar with the airplane, and had found flight and maintenance manuals on board. In addition, the previous squadron had removed armor plate, guns, and ammo. No one would be likely to use this airplane in a combat role again, but it could be an ideal administrative support airplane for our group. On that basis, I sold the idea to Barney and group operations. Our maintenance guys replaced the bad engine, reinstalled the propeller, ran up both engines, checked radios as well as instruments, and found everything operational.

Before flying this airplane for the first time, I wanted to be sure the landing gear system worked properly. The crew chief was far ahead of me. He had scrounged a set of jacks and a hydraulic mule from the service group and already had the airplane up on those jacks in a clean spot in our only hangar. The landing gear functioned as advertised with gear doors closing and opening smoothly in the correct sequence. I studied the flight manual, which was quite skimpy in terms of essential information, but it outlined emergency procedures to follow for engine failure, feathering of a propeller, fire in flight, and how to extend the landing gear if the normal system failed.

The crew chief and I decided to make the first flight with me in the left seat since there were no volunteers. Our preparations were adequate. We fired up both engines, cycled the radios, and received permission to high-speed taxi down the active runway to give me a feel for acceleration and braking. Now there were only two unknowns—whether the new engine would accept full takeoff power and could the guy in the left seat get the airplane airborne and back on the runway safely. At the absolute end of the runway, I held the brakes, ran both engines up to 30 inches of manifold pressure, rechecked gauges in the green, released brakes, and moved throttles smoothly to full power. Acceleration without armor plate, guns, or ammo was impressive. We were off within 2,000 feet of runway. The B-25, which I flew for 10 years in all weather conditions, comes close to being the most responsive to a delicate touch of all aircraft I have flown over some 60 years. I felt at home immediately. We wanted to put time on the factory new engine at fairly high power settings. While waiting for engine temperatures to come back to normal levels indicating the engine was breaking in correctly, I flew landing patterns well above the airfield with gear and flaps down to confirm pattern speeds. I also needed a precise final approach airspeed because this airplane was much lighter without armor plate, guns, and ammo. I flew a final traffic pattern in the landing configuration, leveled off, brought the nose up, reduced power slowly, and held the landing attitude until the airplane stalled. Now I had good numbers for final approach and over-the-fence speeds. I flew a slightly larger pattern for this first landing so we could stabilize airspeeds, note power settings, and select an approach angle which would allow me to flare with power in the overrun for a smooth nose-high touchdown in the first 1,000 feet. That happened in large part because the airspeeds were perfect. The last piece to the puzzle was to decide when to fly the nose wheel down to the runway. This procedure had to begin before the elevator lost effectiveness or the nose would fall some 15 feet to the runway risking collapse of a relatively fragile nose-wheel strut. The crew chief and I built a set of checklists for those in the group who would maintain or fly the B-25. I flew with one pilot from each unit. They were responsible to familiarize their guys. The crew chief followed a similar procedure in assembling a maintenance team. Our checkout procedures worked well. Until the war ended, the 57th flew that B-25 without an accident or incident over the Mediterranean to Malta, Cairo, Nice, Tripoli, Rome, and Naples.

We were heading towards our second Italian winter. There were differences. We had made much progress. The Wehrmacht had been dislodged finally from high ground north of Naples and pushed beyond Rome past the Arno River cities of Pisa and Florence to the Appenines where their stubborn defense of mountainous terrain would again delay significant Allied advances to Bologna and the Po Valley until spring 1945.

After the war, I was assigned as the first Air Force instructor (since Gen Hap Arnold in 1939) on the staff and faculty in the department of Tactics at the Cavalry School, Fort Riley, Kansas. In reviewing my experience in Italy to find examples to explain the basic principles of airpower, I came to appreciate the wisdom of our air commanders who retained control of all air units in the theater.

Instead of allocating the air assets to various Army units, planners applied our resources against the enemy in accordance with these principles. First, establish and maintain air superiority. Second, interdict the enemy's logistic capability and lines of communication. Third, provide close air support (CAS) to our own ground forces in direct contact with enemy forces.

With the Luftwaffe only an intermittent threat to Allied air superiority in the Italian theater, we focused on attacking his logistic base especially lines of communication from Germany through the Brenner Pass and the Po Valley to minimize resupply of his defense forces. Except for Salerno and Anzio beachheads, Allied forces had not requested application of airpower in the role of CAS of troops in contact with enemy forces. Now the American Tenth Mountain Division, determined to break through German defense of high ground north of the Arno River, wanted fighter-bomber units available on airborne alert to provide accurate, heavy firepower against dug-in enemy positions. Army and air commanders approved the concept in a top-level meeting. Implementation was delegated to a team composed of the Tenth Mountain Division operations staff and operations representatives of those fighter groups tasked for close support. We had delivered firepower earlier in the Italian campaign close to our own troops but only with clearly identified targets and known friendly troop positions. In mountains north of the Arno River, it would be difficult to mark enemy targets or know with certainty the position of our own units.

The effort to provide more accurate CAS included such equipment as an Army jeep equipped with air and ground radios and the addition of an experienced fighter pilot (either a flight commander or operations officer) from a participating squadron to act as the forward air controller (FAC). His job would be to communicate with frontline division command posts about their priority targets and pass on accurate descriptions and location coordinates as well as information on the closest friendly troops to an airborne P-47 formation. The tough part was to mark the target with smoke for the P-47 leader. That exercise usually required repetition to be certain the target remained identified. Twelve fighter squadrons tasked for close support operations took turns deploying the FAC to frontline units engaged in the ground battle. The air commander reserved the right to reallocate airpower assets to air superiority or interdiction targets. My turn to be the FAC came in January 1945. The Tenth Mountain Division had trained in winter conditions. They were at home in bad weather on slippery slopes and knew how to operate on snowshoes. All were proficient skiers. Comfortable in mountainous terrain, they were able to pressure the Wehrmacht enough to force a slow, steady retreat. During winter 1944, the Germans held high ground, sustaining the stalemate, until the Allies mounted effective operations in better weather. We developed new operating procedures to respond to close air support requests in timely fashion. Normally, armed recce missions to Brenner Pass and Po Valley targets consisted of 12 or 16 ships. Approaching the Arno River, the mission leader checked in with the FAC who would assign popup targets (if any) to one four-ship section. In most cases, the remaining 12-ship formation would continue to the Po Valley. Another option was to include CAS missions as part of a specific ground offensive operation and schedule four-ship sections each day on airborne alert to be available when needed.

I remember reporting for FAC duty to the frontline division command post. I joined the division staff meeting at night in total darkness, convinced that a productive result under such circumstances was impossible. I underestimated my hosts. With flashlights for illumination, they pinpointed current positions on detailed maps, outlined the next day's objectives, and assigned potential targets for the P-47s allocated to the close support mission. Professional and efficient, primitive accommodations available on the front did not deter them. I found it difficult to adjust to visual limitations at ground level. Although the learning curve was steep, I found a way to relate specific positions in mountainous terrain to available maps.

A standard P-40 bomb load was two 250-pounders carried on fuselage centerline. The P-40 wing stations could not carry weapons or fuel tanks without major redesign of the entire weapon system. The P-47 carried two 500-pounders easily, one on each wing station. In its evolution as the most effective fighter-bomber of the war, we added two and one-half inch rockets with plastic tubes but found that accuracy was poor due to deformation of tubes in flight. It was common to have one of six rockets perform an aerobatic loop instead of tracking to the target. Accuracy improved when metal rails replaced plastic tubes. Anticipating the need for more firepower, we tested 1,000-pound bombs, one on each wing station. Our armament section modified bomb racks for the larger bomb.

After World War II, the Air Force assigned weapons test and development to a specific organization capable of doing the right things to marry weapons with air vehicles to assure aerodynamic compatibility. In winter 1944, combat units in Europe did not have access to that kind of data unless we developed it on our own. Our testing was reduced to finding whether or not the air vehicle could get off the runway with full fuel and two big bombs, whether the bombs would release safely and reliably from wing stations, and what sight adjustments were needed to hit a target.

My P-47 was new and fast with a smooth-running engine that performed well on a morning mission to the Po Valley. Flak was heavy and accurate as usual. On landing, half the flight had damage. For the first time in several missions, I had escaped. For the test, both bombs were unfused. On run-up—everything was normal—gauges were in the green and the engine was smooth and responsive. At full throttle, manifold pressure was a tad low but I hit the water injection switch anyway. The engine surged normally. I released brakes, but my acceleration peaked before reaching takeoff speed. Unable to stop or fly before the end of the runway, I jettisoned the bombs and leaped into the air with ease. After landing, a careful inspection revealed bullet holes in the fuselage skin and internal punctures in the turbocharger that explained the critical loss in acceleration. My airplane had not escaped damage on that morning trip to the Po Valley.

Another set of bombs on a different airplane gave us the anticipated outcome. After takeoff, I accelerated to climb speed, flew past Napoleon's exile island of Elba toward Corsica, and set up a dive-bombing pattern to those isolated rocks we used for bombing practice when we flew from Alto. Using the release airspeed and sight picture that worked well with smaller bombs, I put both 1,000-pound bombs on target. Now we had increased the capability of the P-47 to destroy a wider range of targets and inflict more damage.

During early spring 1944, while operating from Corsica, we modified several airplanes in each squadron with color cameras in the wing pylons to record actual battle damage for use with the documentary movie, *Thunderbolt*, directed by William Wyler. The movie focused on the excellent air-to-ground work by the 57th Fighter Group during Operation Strangle. We found the photos valuable in assessing mission effectiveness, especially the need to restrike important targets. Long after the *Thunderbolt* film was finished, the modified pylons continued to be a positive combat tool that we used through the rest of the air-to-ground war.

We had learned how to avoid many of the German flak batteries en route to target areas. Over the front lines, the Brenner Pass, and certain parts of the Po Valley, the Germans had become more accurate with 88-mm guns using proximity fuses set to explode as shells came close rather than only on contact. Our world had become more dangerous. Even though the Wehrmacht was retreating across all fronts in Europe, German forces were still capable of major offensive operations like the Battle of the Bulge in the Ardennes, and the famous siege of Bastogne during terrible flying weather in December 1944. The end of this Second World War was no longer in doubt. The Allies would certainly prevail, but the German ability to fight the defensive battle with ferocious stubbornness would persist until its final days.

In this last Italian winter of the war, clouds layered to 20,000 feet often characterized typical wet, cold weather. Although we did not have an instrument recovery system on the ground or in the airplanes, we were still able to fly effective missions despite pervasive instrument conditions. If cloud tops were low enough to let us identify the Appenines' peaks south of Bologna and the Alps near Brenner Pass, we could find Po Valley, pick safe headings, and usually descend with reasonable room and visibility to find, bomb, and strafe targets. The Germans did not expect us to fly in such weather. Also we had a target option if cloud layers obscured mountain tops.

A primitive radio direction finding system allowed two or more radio transmitters to pinpoint the formation and provide headings to Bologna where we would release bombs on a countdown. Railroad marshalling yards in Bologna were the target of choice. It was a matter of luck, certainly, but we did some real damage at least once with this system.

In instrument conditions, the key survival skills were leaders who could fly smoothly, think clearly, hold accurate headings, and keep track of time down to seconds. Wingmen had to have the concentration and faith to hold close formation for extended periods in heavy weather. When it was time to head home from Po Valley, we rejoined in four-ship sections to climb on top of the clouds, collect the three or four sections of aircraft, orient ourselves with mountain peaks for the return heading, then start back to Grosseto. Grosseto's ground radio transmitter had direction-finding capability. Within range, the tower operator could determine the compass reading of our transmissions and tell us when we passed the airfield. At that point, it was safe to lose altitude on that outbound heading over the Mediterranean Sea.

My technique in penetrating the overcast was to place the three or four sections in trail flying close formation. Below the clouds or at a specific altitude, I rolled into a 30-degree right bank for 90 degrees of turn then rolled into a 30-degree left bank for 270 degrees of turn to reverse course back to the coastline and then to the airport. In this way, we invented procedures to let us penetrate weather safely to find the airport despite lack of navigational radios or a precision instrument recovery system. Of course, there were many days when weather conditions were literally impossible across the entire Italian peninsula, southern France, and the Mediterranean and Adriatic Seas. During those extended bad weather periods, even sea gulls had the good sense to stay on the ground. I remember coming home on top of a solid undercast hoping to hear Grosseto radio tell me when I was in range that their ceiling was at least 1,000 feet with two miles of visibility underneath the clouds. That was marginal, but anything worse would make recovery of 12 to 16 airplanes, all low on fuel, a dangerous operation. The fact that we always found the field in bad weather without losing anyone is clear evidence that the age of miracles and the power of prayer were both alive and well during that period and are, in my mind, available today to those who pray with faith and a sincere heart.

In these last months of the war, targets in the Po Valley and the Brenner Pass became critical to the ability of the German forces to keep the lines of communication to and from Germany open. If the Allies succeeded in shutting down the road and railroad complex through the Brenner Pass, the Germans could no longer resupply their forces in Italy. More importantly, those forces would be unable to return home except by crossing the Alps—a frightening prospect for every conqueror throughout European history. In their determination to keep the pass viable and open, the Germans literally lined the sides of the Alps looking into the pass with their best guns in quantities we found unbelievable. It became virtually impossible to dive-bomb bridges, trucks, trains, roads, marshalling yards, or power plants effectively without accepting certain damage on nearly every P-47 in the attacking formations. We tried every trick in the book to disguise our intentions but without success. Finally, we sent at least one section with rockets and guns to attack defensive positions on mountainsides just as our dive-bombing sections were rolling in, disrupting concentration of some batteries. Brenner Pass remained the most dangerous target area any air-to-ground fighter pilot had ever seen. The P-47 took those 88- and 40-mm shells, not with impunity, but more often than not, flew back home when any other machine would have quit. We lost airplanes and pilots, certainly, but we destroyed our targets in the Brenner Pass in spite of innovative, stubborn antiaircraft defenses.

I remember one dive-bombing run. After releasing two good bombs on a bridge with excellent results, I decided to continue down the pass retaining my high speed instead of losing it by climbing, our usual tactic. Telling my guys to follow, I went full throttle, saw almost 500 mph on the airspeed indicator, flipped the water injection switch on the throttle to get another seven inches of manifold pressure, and dropped the nose a tad to get even more speed. Now I was flying faster than these gunners expected from the P-47. Their inability to adjust quickly let me literally outrun the shells. I knew there was a break in the mountain on one side that would lead me to one of the Italian lakes away from those persistent gunners. When my five-minute water tank ran dry, I lost the extra thrust and my airplane slowed perceptibly. I looked around in the cockpit for any way to get more speed. With everything full forward, I wound the clock on the panel knowing it was fruitless, but I felt better because I had done everything possible. I found the mountain pass to the lake, continued down to just above the water, eased the throttle back, and looked out on both sides to find the rest of my section still with me rejoining smoothly in formation. We surprised the Germans, hit our targets, and avoided serious damage. It was a great mission. Climbing out of the Po Valley to cross the Appenines on the way home, each of the guys pulled up on my wing to give me a "thumbs up" signal, an unexpected, yet deeply appreciated gesture.

The combination of instrument flying conditions and difficult navigation to and from dangerous targets protected by determined antiaircraft batteries kept stress levels high for all those who had to deal with these tough missions. Barney, Doc Wall, and I looked for ways to relieve the pressure and agreed that a Christmas party might be a wonderful, enjoyable experience for everyone. Counting 1942 at Luke Field, this would be my third year-end holiday away from home. Many of the hardworking enlisted guys would be looking at their third consecutive year in this combat area as would Jim Lynch, executive officer; Fred Ryan, engineering officer; and Peter Mitchell, armament officer. Doc Wall knew the nursing staff at our USA military hospital in Grosseto and would invite them to a formal evening at our officers' club on the beach. I offered to fly the B-25 to Malta to pick up "essential" liquid refreshment for all three squadrons. Malta had been home to worldwide traders throughout its history and had demonstrated on this trip its dedication to perpetuating that legacy by delivering to the airplane the best available product for the best price, on time, as promised.

The flight down the Italian coastline over the beautiful Mediterranean was smooth with a high overcast and good visibility in steady light rain. I chose to cruise at 5,000 feet and trimmed the B-25 carefully so that it held its heading and altitude with little attention from the guy in the left seat. I synchronized the props so that both engines were turning at exactly the same revolutions per minute (RPM). With both engines humming without the annoying audible beat of one out-of-sync prop and the air smooth as silk, it was an opportunity for the guys to get a much-deserved nap. I told my copilot to do the same, that I would wake him in 40 minutes to get a share of that delicious nap while he took care of the flying. We were far from the fighting with no need to search the skies for the Luftwaffe on our way to a night on the town in Valletta. We planned to enjoy the hospitality that Malta extended to traders throughout its history.

Our Christmas party was a wonderful evening. All the officers wore class A uniforms which had been cleaned and pressed especially for this event. The nurses from our hospital were also dressed to the "nines" adding a festive note to the happy occasion. Barney unveiled a plaque that listed the names of all officers who had been part of the Black Scorpions including those lost in action, missing, or prisoners of war. It was a particularly emotional part of the evening as we paid tribute to those who served our country unselfishly.

I had picked a young, bright first lieutenant to be my assistant operations officer. He had been an outstanding flight commander who took care of his guys and demonstrated unusual leadership qualities. P. M. Hall also seemed to be a magnet for 88-mm flak. He had already brought two heavily damaged P-47s back to Grosseto that could not land safely on the runway. He belly-landed both beautifully on the beach at Marina Di Grosseto within walking distance of our squadron building. Before the war ended, "Pranger" Hall would add two more P-47s to his victory list. P. M. survived the war but continued his penchant for crash landing good flying machines and, finally, bailed out of a P-80 in Alaska in frigid winter conditions. He did not survive. The country lost another great fighter pilot.

Not long into the New Year, Barney called all officers to a special meeting. This was unusual. I could not remember when it had happened before. Barney opened with the latest news about Allied problems in Europe with winter weather, the Battle of the Bulge, and the surprising ability of the Germans to mount a viable offensive effort when they should have already depleted their resources. With that out of the way, Barney called me to the front of the room, put me in a brace, and talked about my shocking inability to complete even the simplest tasks on time, but he was willing to give me a second chance. Maj Jim Lynch then read the official order promoting this guy from Boston to major. Barney and Jim each donated a set of gold leaves along with the admonition to get into the proper uniform.

As the calendar moved toward spring, flying weather improved and the pace of operations increased. We needed to upgrade more element and section leaders in accordance with our long-standing policy. Wingmen had to demonstrate the ability to handle additional responsibility. My strongest flight commander had a young, exuberant second lieutenant assigned to him. The lieutenant flew the airplane well, but his lack of good judgment—the ability to think and make good decisions under pressure—marked him as immature, not ready for leadership. His flight commander, believing recent performance merited another shot, scheduled him as element leader on the next mission to Brenner Pass. Watching closely as the formation joined up smoothly in one circle around the field I noticed, with growing concern, the last element closing quickly with too much of a cutoff angle. Fortunately, "Tail-End Charlie" was unable to catch this element leader and that saved his life. In the next seconds, our young element leader, with an excessive closure rate and too much speed, slammed into the section leader's wingman. Both airplanes locked together, fell away from the formation, burst into flames, and hit the ground. Neither pilot had a chance to escape. We lost two pilots and two airplanes in the space of one minute. Fortunately, four unarmed 1,000-pound bombs did not explode in the midair collision or our losses would have been catastrophic. I blame myself for failing to follow my convictions. I learned from that experience that responsible leadership demands tough decisions. I should have intervened, but I did not.

It was clear from Allied advances in Europe that Germany, facing certain defeat, could not continue much longer. Until they ran out of antiaircraft ammo, every mission into Brenner Pass would be dangerous. Heading into the Easter weekend there was no let up in daily missions. Good Friday, 30 March 1945, was just another day with a full schedule. I led the first mission with a crack-of-dawn takeoff, hitting the target area with the sun low in the east and our target for the day still in darkness. I decided to approach from the east, fast, level with the tops of the Alps hoping to take advantage of the early hour to maximize surprise. Passing over a distinctive mountain peak, beyond which was our target railroad complex at the bottom of the pass, we pulled up sharply, rolled inverted into our steep dive, surprised the gunners, managed several direct hits, and escaped down the pass at high speed avoiding much of the heavy flak. Rejoining over my favorite Italian lake, we stayed low searching for rail and road traffic. At that early hour, we found the Germans cheating by staying out past their dawn curfew. We strafed trucks and several motorcycles including one hiding in a haystack that departed just as I was passing by. He was no match for a short burst from my eight guns. We happened upon a train with one steam locomotive moving fast in the open. I rolled in, fixed the pipper on his smoke stack, squeezed another short burst, and watched with amazement when my bullets hit the locomotive dead center, knocking it off the track while the rest of the train continued as if the locomotive were still attached. In a short time, we destroyed the rest of that train and rejoined while climbing out of Po Valley heading to Grosseto. Our second mission to the pass was rolling in on their attack as we reached cruising altitude on the way back to Grosseto. The German flak batteries were fully awake. One of our guys was hit badly. His airplane was still flying but, listening to the radio chatter, there was doubt about making it back to friendly territory before crash landing or bailing out. We got back to Grosseto, landed without incident, debriefed, and waited for the next mission to return. Leroy Hall nursed his damaged P-47 to a point between Bologna and Florence in the Appenines in friendly territory. He bailed out with a good chute but broke a leg landing in the rough terrain. An Army field hospital in the immediate area, alerted to the emergency bail out, picked up Leroy within minutes. We had a message through channels a short time later confirming that Leroy was in that field hospital and his leg would heal normally without surgery.

Doc Wall, worried about one of his guys, asked me if he could borrow a jeep with a driver to visit the hospital, a difficult trip by road. We learned that the hospital, located at the 7,000-foot level, had a functional ski-jump-type airstrip used to airlift patients, other personnel, or supplies. We had a small single engine L-5 in which I was current. There was plenty of daylight left for the two-hour trip. With Doc Wall in the back seat, we flew to Florence and landed at a racetrack to refuel at an Army artillery observation unit. The commander graciously pinpointed the hospital airstrip on a detailed map and reminded me to land into the mountain and depart down the ski jump. The weather was clear with excellent visibility. I found the airstrip easily, circled carefully, and set up my approach to land. As I rolled out on final, a strong crosswind blowing from right to left made it obvious that I could not land on that approach. With full throttle at that high altitude, the L-5 was working hard to hold flying speed just above the treetops. We were holding our own, gaining speed as we turned right to the downwind for a second approach. At that critical moment, the struggling engine quit. I brought the stick back to give us a nose-high landing attitude and we settled into closely packed tree tops, perhaps the best landing I could have made under those conditions. There was no fire, the engine came back almost to my lap. Doc hit the X-shaped cross bar between the seats. No broken bones, but collision with the glare shield forced the rim of my sunglasses to split my left eyelids above and below the eye with no damage to the eye itself. Fortunately, at this remote location, one of the few surgeons capable of delicately reconnecting the myriad of tiny muscles necessary for a functioning eyelid system was available and operated on me successfully. When I awakened after surgery, Doc, Leroy, and I were side by side. My last memory of the accident was the silence after the engine quit as we settled into the trees. Because of the delicate nature of the surgery, I remained in the field hospital until my surgeon was satisfied that no further surgery would be necessary. Doc and Leroy were released in a few days to return by ambulance to Grosseto. That little L-5 is the only airplane I did not bring back to a runway in a flying career that has lasted 60 years and continues to this day with more than 14,000 hours. I suspect the engine was the victim of carburetor icing due to my mismanagement of the carburetor heat control and complicated by operating at the unusual 7,000-foot altitude of that mountain airstrip. It proves the accuracy of a familiar adage, "Aviation is terribly unforgiving of any mistake especially those of the stupid variety." I was under medical observation until the end of April 1945.

When the world learned of the death of President Roosevelt on 13 April, I remember wondering about the impact of that event on the resolution of the peace process following the end of this climactic world war. During the month of April, the three squadrons flew from Villa Franca north of Venice close to Brenner Pass, a location that enabled missions to be flown into Bavaria if required. By the time I returned to flying status at the end of April, our three squadrons came back to Grosseto where we remained through Victory in Europe (VE) day and the celebrations that followed. The 57th Fighter Group, selected to be part of the support package for the invasion of Japan, was on the high seas en route to the Pacific when the Japanese surrendered 15 August 1945. Rerouted to Boston, the group arrived a few days later in time to participate in one of the great celebrations of the twentieth century. I left the group after VE day, arrived in June, processed through Atlantic City, and found myself scheduled to be a FAC in the air support package for the Japanese invasion force. My life expectancy improved dramatically while attending the air ground operations school at Key Field, Mississippi, when Japan quit after two nuclear bombs were dropped at Hiroshima and Nagasaki.

Index

20th Tactical Fighter Wing, 24
324th Fighter Group, 25
337th Fighter Group, 11
51st Fighter Group, 25
57th Fighter Group, 21–22, 25, 28, 47, 58, 67, 70–71, 78–79, 81–82, 88, 96
64th Squadron, 22, 67, 72, 77, 81
99th Fighter Squadron, 26

A-20, 16, 18–20
Abercrombie, Bruce, 26, 48, 59, 76, 78, 82
Africa, 11, 15–16, 19–22, 24, 45, 48, 50, 58, 66, 81
Africa Corps, 16, 20–21, 45, 48
air superiority, 55, 79, 85–86
Aix, 80
Algeria, 20, 25
Allied VI Corps, 68
Alto, 71, 75, 77, 79, 87
Amendola, 48, 58, 60–62, 66–67, 82
American Tenth Mountain Division, 85
Ancona, 61, 82
antiaircraft weapons, 45
Anzio, 68–70, 76, 79, 85
Appenines, 71, 79, 84, 88, 91, 94
Arcola, 67, 69, 71
armed recce, 56, 61, 63, 68, 71, 74, 76, 86
Arno, 71, 76, 79, 84–86
Arno River, 71, 76, 79, 84–86
AT-6, 8–9, 11–12
Atlantic City, 78, 96
Australia, 58

B-17, 78
B-24, 58
B-25, 16, 68, 70, 74, 82–84, 91–92
Bari, 58
Barnum, Maj Bob, 81
Bastia, 69, 71
Bavaria, 45, 96
Bilby, Maj Buck, 22, 24, 46
Black Scorpions, 24, 59, 92
Blednick, George, 26, 48, 52, 59, 82
Bologna, 76, 84, 88–89, 94
Bolsena, Lake, 73
boot camp, 1, 78
Boston, 1, 11, 26, 51, 78, 93, 96

Boston Latin School, 1, 26
Brandon, Gerry, 23
Brenner Pass, 45, 85–86, 88, 90, 93–94, 96
Britain, 55, 58, 60, 65
British Eighth Army, 20, 45, 58
BT-13 Vultee "Vibrator", 5–6
Byrne, Rocky, 23, 27

C-47, 8, 21, 52, 66, 77
C-54, 14–15
Cairo, 16, 18, 20–21, 25, 48, 81, 84
Canada, 58
Capadochino, 66–67
Cape Bon, 13, 20–21, 23–28, 45, 52
Capri, 66
Carefree, 4–5
Carll, Paul, 26, 48, 52, 59, 65, 76, 78, 82
Causeway, 28
celestial navigation, 15
Class 43-A, 1, 11, 26, 48, 61, 76
close air support (CAS), 71, 85–86
Coast Guard Women's Reserves, 78
Corsica, 11, 50, 65, 69, 71, 73–75, 77–82, 87–88

Dale Mabry Field, 14
Davis, Lt Col Ben O., 26
DC-4, 15
D–Day, 79
Denneler, Buck, 51
dive–bombing, 13, 26, 46, 48, 60, 71, 73–74, 80, 87, 90
Duck Butt, 47

Egypt, 22–23
Eighth Air Force, 60
Eighth Army, 20, 45–46, 58
El Fasher, 18–20
El Kabrit, 21
Exon, Capt Art, 48, 53
Exon, Maj Art, 72

Fairlamb, Capt George, 21
fear, 7, 49–52, 79
flak, 46–48, 54–56, 60–61, 65, 74, 87–88, 92, 94
Florence, 71, 84, 94–95
Foggia, 48, 54–55, 58–61, 66
formation flying, 13, 73, 89
Fort Lamy, 18–19

Fort Riley, 84
forward air controller (FAC), 85–86, 96
Frank, Capt Lou, 72, 76, 81
Fudge, Lt Don, 12–14
Fw 190, 21, 73

Glendale, 1
Gold Coast, 15
Grosseto, 80, 82, 92
gunnery, 13
Gustav, 58, 61

Haines, Capt Risley, 27
Hall, 1st Lt P. M. "Pranger", 94
He 111, 82
Hogan, Margaret, 78
Hurricane, 57

Italy, 2, 4, 6–8, 11–12, 14, 16, 18, 20, 22, 24, 26, 28, 45–63, 65–68, 70, 72, 74, 76, 78, 80–82, 84, 86, 88, 90, 92, 94, 96

Japan, 96
Ju 52, 21
Ju 88, 23, 27
Jug, 65

Kairouan, 22, 25, 52
Kano, 18–19
Keller, Gus, 26, 48, 60, 82
Key Field, 96
Khartoum, 18–20
Kowalski, Gene, 57

L-5, 95–96
Lafayette Esquadrille, 75, 79
Lagos, 16, 21
Lake Bolsena, 73
Lampedusa, 53
Libya, 22–23
Liebing, Ed, 68
lines of communication, 85, 90
logistic capability, 85
Los Angeles, 1
Lucas, Maj Gen John P., 68
Luftwaffe, 22–26, 55, 59–60, 72, 76, 81–82, 85, 92
Luke Field, 8, 48, 91
Lynch, Jim, 91, 93

Malta, 28, 46, 58, 66, 84, 91–92
Manfredonia, 60
Marana, 5, 7–9
Marcum, "Stovebolt", 23
Marina Di Grosseto, 81–82, 92

Marseille, 80
Martin, Roy, 2
Maxwell Air Force Base, 24, 48
Me 109, 24–25, 27, 56, 60, 63, 73
Me 110, 21, 23
Messina Straits, 45–49, 55
Miami, 14
Middleditch, Lyman, 23
Milano, 76
Mitchell, Peter, 91
Mobbs, George, 23
Monte Cassino, 67–68, 70, 75, 79
Montgomery, Gen Bernard L., 16, 45
Mostar, 59–60
Mount Etna, 45, 56
Murphy, Arthur, 11

Naples, 7, 54–56, 58, 66–67, 69, 77–78, 84
navigation, 15, 91
Neese, Charlie, 26
Novy, Capt Jim, 76, 78, 81
Nuding, Bill, 26–27

Ombrone, 81
Oran, 78

P-40, 11–13, 15–16, 18, 20, 23–26, 46–47, 49–51, 56, 62–63, 65, 68, 81, 86
P-47, 49, 63, 65–66, 68–70, 72, 77, 80–82, 85–88, 90, 94
Pachino, 28, 46, 48
Palermo, 45
Pantelleria, 26
Patton, Gen George S. Jr., 45
photo recce, 71
pierced steel planking (PSP), 46, 71
pipper, 54–56, 63, 73–74, 94
Ploesti, 60
Po Valley, 45, 65, 69, 71, 76, 78–79, 81, 84–91, 94
Pompeii, 69

radio navigation, 15
Ranger, 23, 48, 81
Raskin, Moe, 48, 60, 62, 82
Reade, Chad, 72, 80
Rocco Bernardo, 57
Rome, 58, 68, 71–74, 76, 79, 84
Rommel, Gen Erwin, 16
Royal Air Force (RAF), 27–28, 47, 57, 62, 76
Ryan, Fred, 91

Salerno, 56–57, 85
Salisbury, Col Art, 24, 46, 65
Santa Ana Army Air Base, 1
Sarajevo, 59
Sarasota, 11–12, 48
Scordia, 47, 53–56
Scottsdale, 4
Sfax, 22
Shore, Dinah, 9
Sicily, 11, 14, 21–22, 24, 26–28, 45–47, 50, 52, 55–56, 66
Sousse, 22
South Africa, 58
SPARS, 78
Spitfire, 25, 27–28
Split Harbor, 59
Stearman, 3, 5
Suez Canal, 21

Tanner, Lieutenant, 5–7
Tenth Mountain Division, 85–86
Termoli, 58, 67
Thunderbird One, 1, 8

Thunderbird Two, 4–5
Thunderbolt, 88
Trinidad, 15
Tripoli, 28, 52, 84
Tunis, 25, 48
Tunisia, 22–23, 25
Turin, 76
Tuskegee, Alabama, 26

United States, 58–59, 77–78

Valletta, 92
Vesuvius, 67–70, 81
Victory in Europe (VE), 96
Villa Franca, 96

Wadi Haifa, 18, 21
Wall, Lester A. (Doc), 82, 91, 95
Watson, Lieutenant, 7
Wehrmacht, 56, 79, 84, 86, 88
Wethersfield, England, 24
Wilson, George, 82
Wyler, William, 88

Yellownose Squadron, 70